Science and Religion

PREVIOUSLY PUBLISHED RECORDS OF BUILDING BRIDGES SEMINARS

The Road Ahead: A Christian-Muslim Dialogue,
Michael Ipgrave, Editor (London: Church House, 2002)

*Scriptures in Dialogue: Christians and Muslims Studying the Bible and the Qur'ān
Together*, Michael Ipgrave, Editor (London: Church House, 2004)

Bearing the Word: Prophecy in Biblical and Qur'ānic Perspective,
Michael Ipgrave, Editor (London: Church House, 2005)

Building a Better Bridge: Muslims, Christians, and the Common Good,
Michael Ipgrave, Editor (Washington, DC: Georgetown University Press, 2008)

Justice and Rights: Christian and Muslim Perspectives, Michael Ipgrave, Editor
(Washington, DC: Georgetown University Press, 2009)

Humanity: Texts and Contexts: Christian and Muslim Perspectives,
Michael Ipgrave and David Marshall, Editors
(Washington, DC: Georgetown University Press, 2011)

*Communicating the Word: Revelation, Translation, and Interpretation
in Christianity and Islam*, David Marshall, Editor
(Washington, DC: Georgetown University Press, 2011)

For further information about the Building Bridges seminars, please visit
http://berkleycenter.georgetown.edu/resources/networks/building_bridges.

Science and Religion

CHRISTIAN AND MUSLIM PERSPECTIVES

*A record of the eighth Building Bridges seminar
convened by the Archbishop of Canterbury
Bahçeşehir University, Istanbul, June 16–18, 2009*

DAVID MARSHALL, Editor

GEORGETOWN UNIVERSITY PRESS
Washington, DC

Library of Congress Cataloging-in-Publication Data

Building Bridges Seminar (8th : 2009 : Bahçesehir University)
Science and religion : Christian and Muslim perspectives : a record of the eighth Building Bridges Seminar convened by the Archbishop of Canterbury, Bahçesehir University, Istanbul, 16–18 June 2009 / edited by David Marshall.
    p.   cm.
  Includes bibliographical references and index.
  ISBN 978-1-58901-914-0 (pbk. : alk. paper)
  1. Religion and science—Congresses.   2. Christianity—Doctrines—Congresses.
3. Islam—Doctrines—Congresses.   4. Bible—Criticism, interpretation, etc.—Congresses.
5. Koran—Criticism, interpretation, etc.—Congresses.   6. Christianity and other religions—Islam—Congresses.   7. Islam—Relations—Christianity—Congresses.
I. Marshall, David, Rev. II. Title.
BL240.3.B85   2009
262.2'7—dc23
2011041625

♾ This book is printed on acid-free paper meeting the requirements of the American National Standard for Permanence in Paper for Printed Library Materials.

19   18   17   16   15   14   13   12   9   8   7   6   5   4   3   2
First printing

Printed in the United States of America

Contents

Participants

ALPARSLAN AÇIKGENÇ
Professor of Philosophy, Fatih University, Istanbul

DENIS ALEXANDER
Director, Faraday Institute for Science and Religion, St. Edmund's College, Cambridge, UK

OSMAN BAKAR
Professor of Islamic Thought and Civilization, International Institute of Islamic Thought and Civilization (ISTAC), Kuala Lumpur

NAHIDE BOZKURT
Professor of Theology, Ankara University

JOHN HEDLEY BROOKE
Emeritus Professor of Science and Religion, University of Oxford, UK

EMMANUEL CLAPSIS
Archbishop Iakovos Professor of Systematic Theology, Holy Cross Greek Orthodox School of Theology, Brookline, Massachusetts

VINCENT CORNELL
Asa Griggs Candler Professor of Arabic and Islamic Studies, Department of Middle East and South Asian Studies, Emory University, Atlanta, Georgia

AHMAD DALLAL
Provost and Professor of History, American University of Beirut

ELLEN F. DAVIS
Amos Ragan Kearns Distinguished Professor of Bible and Practical Theology, Duke University, Durham, North Carolina

CELIA DEANE-DRUMMOND
Professor in Theology and the Biosciences, and Director of the Centre for
Religion and the Biosciences, University of Chester, UK

JOHN J. DEGIOIA
President, Georgetown University, Washington, DC

MARWA ELSHAKRY
Associate Professor of History of Science, Columbia University, New York

SHERINE HAMDY
Assistant Professor, Department of Anthropology, Brown University,
Providence, Rhode Island

DŽEVAD HODŽIĆ
Professor of Ethics, Faculty of Islamic Studies, Sarajevo

JOSIAH IDOWU-FEARON
Bishop of Kaduna, Nigeria

IBRAHIM KALIN
Director, Seta Foundation for Political, Economic, and Social Research,
Ankara

BEKIR KARLIGA
Professor of Islamic Philosophy, Bahçeşehir University, Istanbul

FELIX KÖRNER
Director of the Institute for the Study of Religions and Cultures, Pontifical
Gregorian University, Rome

JANE DAMMEN MCAULIFFE
President, Bryn Mawr College, Bryn Mawr, Pennsylvania

MUSTANSIR MIR
Professor of Islamic Studies, Youngstown State University, Youngstown, Ohio

EBRAHIM MOOSA
Associate Professor of Islamic Studies, Department of Religion,
Duke University, Durham, North Carolina

MICHAEL NAZIR-ALI
Bishop of Rochester, Church of England

NG KAM WENG
Research Director, Kairos Research Centre, Kuala Lumpur

MEHMET PAÇACI
Professor, Ankara University

CHRISTOPH SCHWÖBEL
Professor of Systematic Theology, University of Tübingen, Germany

RECEP ŞENTÜRK
Professor of Sociology, Fatih University, Istanbul

MICHAEL WELKER
Professor of Systematic Theology, University of Heidelberg, Germany

ROWAN WILLIAMS
Archbishop of Canterbury, Church of England

Introduction

David Marshall

This volume is a record of the eighth Building Bridges seminar, on the theme "Science and Religion: Christian and Muslim Perspectives," convened by the Archbishop of Canterbury and held from June 16 to 18, 2009, at Bahçeşehir University, Istanbul. The seminar, following an established Building Bridges pattern, consisted of a day of public lectures followed by two days of private sessions attended just by seminar participants, a group of Muslim and Christian scholars from several different nations.

The opening address given on the first day by Archbishop Rowan Williams is included in this volume as "Building Bridges in Istanbul." After some remarks on the Building Bridges dialogue process, he briefly introduces the seminar's theme, insisting that the histories of both Christianity and Islam show that it is "a complete falsehood to suggest that there is an intrinsic hostility between the scientific worldview and religious faith."

The public lectures that then followed offered wide-ranging accounts of broad themes in the interface between science and religion, past and present; edited versions of some of these lectures are included in part I ("Surveys"). In his essay "Science and the Christian Tradition: A Brief Overview," John Hedley Brooke notes that for historians of science "there is a wonderful richness and diversity in the relations between different sciences and different religious traditions. There is no such thing as *the* relationship between science and religion and there has certainly been no such thing as *the* relationship between science and Christianity. It has been constructed and reconstructed in many different ways within different Christian traditions and in many different social and political contexts." Brooke demonstrates this richness and diversity in a survey stretching from the church fathers to the modern era.

In his essay "Science and Religion in the History of Islam" Ahmad Dallal makes the similar point that the work of Muslim scientists in the classical period was "a complex phenomenon that does not lend itself to single track and static explanations." He demonstrates how the need to determine the qibla or direction for prayer raised acute questions about the relationship between mathematical knowledge and religious authority. "The significance of the qibla debate is that precise epistemological discussions filtered down to the most sensitive matter of prayer, raising in no uncertain terms the question of intellectual authority within Islam's most sacred space." Dallal goes on to consider the work of three significant Muslim thinkers working in the interface between scientific and religious concerns: al-Bīrūnī, al-Ghazālī, and Fakhr al-Dīn al-Rāzī.

With Denis Alexander's essay "Science and Religious Belief in the Modern World: Challenges and Opportunities," the focus moves to more recent debate. He identifies three streams of thought—postmodernism, the so-called New Atheism, and fundamentalism—in each case exploring both the challenges raised for the dialogue between science and religious belief as well as the opportunities offered. Alexander concludes by echoing the sentiments of the Christian evolutionary biologist Francis Collins, who describes his work as a scientist as "a work of discovery which can also be a form of worship."

The focus of the private sessions on the second and third days of the seminar was the study of texts, chosen after consultation with a number of participants, which were first introduced through short plenary presentations and then discussed in small groups. Part II, "Texts and Commentaries," gives a selection of the texts discussed, together with the presentations introducing them and questions for further reflection. Proceeding in chronological sequence, the first texts to be considered are from the Bible and the Qur'ān. The inclusion of scriptural texts did not arise from a view that they are in some literalist sense "about science and religion" but rather out of a concern to identify fundamental scriptural bearings toward God's creation that it seemed important to consider. Because of its focus on the first chapter of the book of Genesis, Michael Welker's lecture is included at this point, following the commentary by Ellen Davis on the biblical texts. Mustansir Mir provides comments on the Qur'ānic texts.

After these scriptural texts we progress to classical Christian and Islamic authors, looking at passages from Basil of Caesaraea, Gregory of Nyssa, and

Augustine of Hippo (with commentary by Emmanuel Clapsis), and al-Ghazālī and Ibn Rushd (with commentary by Osman Bakar). The following section focuses on Charles Darwin. With the seminar being held in 2009, the two-hundredth anniversary of his birth, it was natural that some time was given to considering the significance of his thought for the science–religion dialogue. A selection of relevant passages from Darwin's writings is followed by essays by John Hedley Brooke and Marwa Elshakry; Brooke combines biographical information and comments on the texts while Elshakry discusses early Arabic views of Darwin. Finally, we move into the twentieth century with passages from two highly influential Egyptian Muslim writers, Sayyid Quṭb and Shaykh Muḥammad Mutwallī al-Shaʿrāwī (with commentary by Sherine Hamdy), and two significant texts from Pope John Paul II (with commentary by Celia Deane-Drummond).

Together with the selection of texts presented here, the main contents of this volume are thus revised versions of the presentations that provided the framework for dialogue at the seminar, and it is hoped that this material will be of value both to those new to this field and to those more familiar with its complexities. Within this formal framework there was naturally also a great deal of conversation, in plenary sessions and in small groups. It has not been possible to offer a systematic account of these conversations here, but in this volume's afterword Archbishop Rowan Williams reflects on some of the main themes that recurred as the dialogue unfolded over the three days of the seminar.

Acknowledgments

For some years, Georgetown University has generously supported Building Bridges and has made possible the publication of volumes recording the seminars. Sincere thanks are once again due to the president of Georgetown University, Dr. John J. DeGioia, for his unfailing commitment to this initiative. The process of writing this volume has been somewhat delayed, and along the way the patient support and advice of several people has been essential. Many thanks to Archbishop Rowan Williams; to Richard Brown and the staff of Georgetown University Press; and to Tom Banchoff, director of the Berkley Center for Religion, Peace, and World Affairs at Georgetown University.

Thanks are also due to those who advised on the selection of texts discussed at the seminar, particularly John Hedley Brooke, Ahmad Dallal, Celia Deane-Drummond, Marwa Elshakry, and Alister McGrath.

Note on Translations of the Bible and the Qur'ān

When not indicated otherwise in the notes, the translations of the Qur'ān in this volume are either from M. A. S. Abdel Haleem, *The Qur'an: A New Translation* (Oxford: Oxford University Press, 2004), or are the author's own translation, and translations of the Bible are either from the New Revised Standard Version or are the author's own translation.

Building Bridges in Istanbul

ROWAN WILLIAMS

I WANT TO BEGIN by thanking Bahçeşehir University very heartily for the generous welcome and expert cooperation that they have given to us in the planning of this seminar.[1] We are very honored to be received with such warmth, and we look forward to spending time in this environment in the days that lie ahead.

By way of introduction I want to say a few words first about the nature of the Building Bridges seminar and then about the subject matter that we shall be addressing over the coming days. First of all, the Building Bridges seminar itself. This is the eighth of the seminars under this title. The first was convened by my predecessor as Archbishop of Canterbury, George Carey, very shortly after the tragic events of September 11. The Building Bridges seminar grew out of a vision that scholars of Christianity and Islam ought to be meeting together, in an atmosphere without political pressure, to discuss at depth the concerns, priorities, and insights that they wish to share with each other in the hope that this discussion might have an impact on the wider world. The seminar has never sought to be a major public event. We have not issued statements, but we have published our proceedings, the papers and the lectures that have been given on these occasions. The main focus of each seminar has been that we should form trusting relationships with each other and that we should be able to take something of that trust and confidence in each other back to our own institutions and our own religious bodies.

What has been perhaps most distinctive about the seminar from the beginning has been an emphasis on our method. We have always sought to do our business by working from the sacred texts of Islam and Christianity. We have concentrated a great deal of our energy on reading our sacred texts together in the belief that, as I have sometimes put it, when you see someone else reading their own sacred scripture, you see their face turned toward God.

1

That is a very good basis for trust, confidence, and friendship as the discussion unfolds. So for each of these seminars we have selected a number of texts from our scriptures, as well as some from commentaries, as the basis of discussion. Thus, we have not sought to address topics or issues in the abstract but as they arise from the central texts of revelation as we see them in our different faiths. I believe that this has been a fruitful and challenging method to follow, one that has allowed us to enter some areas of reflection not often explored in inter faith discussion. I certainly believe that this method has helped to deepen and reinforce the links of trust and friendship between us.

For each of the seminars we have sought to draw from a wide range of representatives of Christianity and Islam. We have sought people from across the globe and from different kinds of background and conviction within the Christian and the Muslim worlds. Over these years, we have also been privileged to take the seminar to different settings. We have met in Doha, Washington, Sarajevo, Singapore, and Rome. We have been supported in all of this work with enormous faithfulness and generosity by Georgetown University, and I want to pay public tribute to President DeGioia and his colleagues for their support and that welcome. We have hoped that in taking the seminar to different places around the world we might be able to model for different contexts what is involved in constructive encounter between Muslims and Christians to show that it is possible to have deep, honest, and constructive conversation even about the most difficult questions.

We have been greatly helped in several of the seminars by the presence of scholars from Turkey. It was therefore a very great delight when, at our last seminar, it was suggested that we might consider holding the Building Bridges seminar in Istanbul. I am particularly grateful to our Turkish colleagues and friends for their encouragement and their inspiration in this respect. We were happy to come to Istanbul, partly because we were aware of the depth and sophistication with which questions about Islam and modernity are being addressed in this context. The quality of the scholarship and reflection that our Turkish colleagues have shown encouraged us to believe that this was indeed a place in which we might feel ourselves at home in this kind of discussion. We are aware that at the moment in Turkey questions about Islam and higher education, about science and faith, and about the role of faith in public life are very live concerns. We hope to learn from the discussions currently going on here.

I want now to say a few words about the subject matter of the conference we are about to begin. It is no secret that, in this anniversary year of Charles Darwin, questions about the relationship between science and religious faith have once again become very current. In recent years, certainly in the English-speaking world but also more widely, a number of very fierce attacks on religious faith have been published by those who consider themselves the heirs or disciples of Charles Darwin. However, many people in several religious communities have responded by saying that the legacy of Charles Darwin is by no means uniformly hostile to religious faith, that we need to understand better the questions that he was raising. Indeed, we need to understand better the whole nature of the challenge that scientific research poses to theology.

Both Christianity and Islam have been challenged in various ways by the development of modern science. I say "modern science" because of course we are all aware of the extraordinary contribution to the history of science made by Islamic civilization, and we are aware of the significance of some aspects of Christian philosophy and metaphysics in shaping the scientific worldview in Western Europe. It is a complete falsehood to suggest that there is an intrinsic hostility between the scientific worldview and religious faith. The histories of both our religious traditions make that abundantly clear.

However, modern science has developed in a number of ways that have at times appeared hostile to religious faith. Many modern scientists have supposed that when they do their scientific research they are speaking from a position of, you might say, total synoptic understanding of how the world works so that the basic, most fundamentally true way of talking about the world is in terms of material interaction. That reductive approach is perhaps the most generative of conflict between scientists and people of faith, at least as the media and popular intellectual communication presents it. I make no apology for saying that the scholars represented at this meeting will all wish to challenge the false simplicities of such a picture and the reductive approach that it represents. We are all conscious of the danger of a totalizing approach from materialistic science that blocks out other kinds of question. That is not the way for human flourishing to develop.

These are current questions. They are acute questions in the Western European and North American intellectual worlds, but these questions are also increasingly recognized in other parts of the world. Both Muslim and Christian scholars are engaged in responding to the challenges of our day, but Muslim and Christian scholars engaged in this work have not as yet found all that many opportunities to talk to each other about their responses to these challenges. So our hope is that this meeting may help to open up still further conversations and exchanges in this area.

The challenging and intriguing conversation that we shall be pursuing has great significance for the whole of our global civilization. I choose the word "global" advisedly. I know how very deeply the study of civilizations is part of the distinctive work of this university. I also know how very damaging the talk can be of a clash of civilizations in our world. Global civilization will never be one single thing, obliterating all local differences, but at the very least it is a civil and civilized conversation between people of different cultures and commitments devoted to the good of the human race and, for people of faith, the good of the human race as created for relationship with Almighty God. It is in that hope and that vision that we begin our work.

Note

1. This is an edited version of the address given by Archbishop Rowan Williams at the opening of the seminar.

PART I

Surveys

Science and the Christian Tradition

A Brief Overview

John Hedley Brooke

Two stories are commonly told about the relations between science and Christianity. At one extreme the story is all about conflict.[1] The trial of Galileo by the Roman Catholic Church and continuing battles between Darwinians and creationists often make the headlines. At the other extreme we find the contrary claim that there would have been no modern science without Christianity.[2] This sometimes surprising argument has taken different forms, but it depends on a simple idea: that a search for laws of nature only makes sense if creation has been ordered by a rational Creator, by a transcendent lawgiver. Isaac Newton saw this connection when he suggested that science had only prospered in monotheistic cultures. The mathematics of the solar system pointed to a deity no less brilliant than Newton himself, or in Newton's own words a "deity very well skilled in mechanics and geometry."[3]

The many fine achievements of Muslim scientists from the ninth to the sixteenth centuries, recently discussed by Ahmad Dallal, are consistent with Newton's remark.[4] Understanding the universe as a creation certainly did regulate thinking in much of early modern science. But the view that Christianity alone provided the necessary presuppositions is an exaggeration, recently classified as a "myth" in the book *Galileo Goes to Jail and Other Myths about Science and Religion*.[5] For historians of science there is a wonderful richness and diversity in the relations between different sciences and different religious traditions. There is no such thing as *the* relationship between science and religion, and there has certainly been no such thing as *the* relationship between science and Christianity.[6] It has been constructed and reconstructed in many different ways within different Christian traditions and in many different social and political contexts.

Diversity is found, for example, among the fathers of the Christian church. Some like Tertullian saw little value in the study of nature and in the achievements of the Greek natural philosophers: "Away with all attempts to produce a mottled Christianity of Stoic, Platonic, and dialectic composition!" Tertullian wanted "no curious disputation after possessing Christ Jesus, no inquisition after enjoying the gospel!" Having that faith, "we desire no further belief."[7] Tertullian was not typical of the church fathers, although all believed there were higher priorities than the investigation of nature. One of the reasons given by Basil of Caesarea for disregarding pagan scientific speculations was grounded in the observation that the Greek philosophers disagreed among themselves: no sooner was one theory proposed than it was succeeded by another and then another. What confidence, then, could be placed in them?[8] Interestingly, that argument from the history of science still surfaces from time to time in critiques of realist philosophies of science.

In St. Augustine, however, there is a more positive estimate of the value of physical science. There will always be more urgent matters for the Christian disciple than the study of nature, but Augustine also warns that it would be embarrassing and disgraceful for Christians to be caught out talking nonsense on scientific topics. In his commentary on Genesis, Augustine even drew on Stoic philosophy to solve an exegetical problem. The Stoic concept of "seeds" allowed him to say that, when the world was first created, it was complete— and yet not completely complete. It would take time for living things to develop from the seeds implanted by the Creator. With reference to the origins of humankind, he put it like this: God "created man in the sense that he made the man who was to be, that is, the causal principle of man to be created, not the actuality of man already created."[9] A consequence of this approach was that the six "days" of the Creation narrative were not to be taken literally.[10] In Augustine's understanding of potentiality in the world, there is a greater subtlety than we sometimes find among the young-earth creationists of today. The critical point, however, is that Augustine illustrates an attitude toward the sciences that has reappeared many times in the history of Western Christianity. It manifests itself in what I like to call the selective role of religious belief because Christians (and they are not alone in this) have usually been happy to select from current bodies of science those features that reinforce their faith, dispensing with the rest. As Augustine himself put it, "if those who are called philosophers, especially the Platonists, have said things that are indeed true and are well accommodated to our faith, they should not be feared; rather what they have said should be taken from them as from unjust possessors and converted to our use."[11] In this respect even pagan knowledge could be the handmaiden of the Christian religion.

A critical moment for the development of Christian theology came in the thirteenth century when European scholars had to meet the intellectual challenge enshrined in the works of Aristotle. It was clear from Arabic translations recently translated into Latin that, more than any other ancient thinker, Aristotle offered a comprehensive system of knowledge that embraced the physical and life sciences. Medieval Christian scholars such as Roger Bacon, who argued that mathematics and science were essential for the church's mission to infidels, were full of admiration. But there was a problem—one that had already been faced by Muslim scholars. Aristotle argued for at least three propositions that were theologically unacceptable: the mortality of the soul, the eternity of the universe, and the planting of all causal agency within nature itself. In response, one of the greatest Christian theologians, Thomas Aquinas, drew from Aristotle all that could lend support to the faith, at the same time rejecting Aristotle's conclusions when they conflicted with what Christians believed from revelation. But Aquinas went further. He aimed to show that Aristotle's reasoning—on the eternity of motion, for example—was not a danger to faith in a Creator. Because the ultimate cause of motion was God, the source of all being, Aquinas could present his theology as a completion of Aristotle's physics. The ends or final causes, which Aristotle placed within nature, could only be fully understood if they were also grounded in a transcendent Providence.

There is a particularly interesting critique of Aristotle that one finds in both Christian and Muslim scholars. This concerns the nature of Aristotle's proofs for propositions about nature. According to Aristotle, the Earth *had* to be at the center of the cosmos because that was its natural place. Move it away and it would return to where it belonged. Similarly, for Aristotle it was impossible that there could be more than one cosmos because if there were two there would have to be two centers. And this would lead to absurdity because a falling object, which must always fall to the center, would be caught between incompatible demands. It would not know which way to turn. If, however, one believed in the omnipotence of God, there was an unwelcome dogmatism in saying that anything *had* to be the case. The argument that nature is organized as it is because it cannot be otherwise surely overlooks the fact that an omnipotent Creator could have chosen to organize the creation differently. In 1277, protesting against arguments that he believed were putting constraints on God's power, the bishop of Paris, Étienne Tempier, famously condemned no fewer than 219 propositions allegedly taught in the arts faculty of the University of Paris.[12] In principle, such theological critiques created the space for a more critical science of nature, and they were to have echoes in seventeenth-century Europe when empirical methods for the study of nature achieved a higher profile.

An example is the French Catholic scholar Marin Mersenne, who in the 1630s was a kind of one-man "Internet," in touch with leading scientists across Europe. Mersenne specifically objected to the idea that the Earth *must* be at the center of the universe. It could have been placed wherever God wished, and it was no use sitting and philosophizing in an armchair to discover where that was.[13] Mersenne showed a willingness to countenance the alternative Copernican system. In England, when Francis Bacon defended the need for experimental methods in science, he attacked the learning of the universities precisely because such learning was too preoccupied with philosophical commentaries on ancient thinkers. If God had been free to make any number of different worlds, then empirical methods were indispensable for discovering which of the many possibilities had actually been instantiated.[14] In Bacon's vision, Christian humility and experimental methods went hand in hand in opposition to the arrogance and practical sterility of scholastic philosophy.

By the seventeenth century, when Bacon and Mersenne were writing, Christianity had been divided by the Reformation associated with Martin Luther and John Calvin. In many ways the expansion of Protestantism favored the expansion of the natural sciences. A critical attitude to the authority of the Catholic Church could lead to greater freedom of thought in the interpretation of nature. Luther had been no friend to Aristotle, describing him as a "Greek buffoon" who had "befooled the Church," "a cursed arrogant, rascally heathen," and "truly a devil . . . a most horrid impostor on mankind."[15] He really liked him! Not surprisingly, Luther attacked Aquinas for having introduced Aristotle's "unchristian, profane, meaningless babblings" into theology.[16] And although Luther was no friend to the astronomical system of Copernicus, it is striking how many of the key players in moving the Earth were Lutherans, including the famous astronomer Johannes Kepler.[17] Catholic scholars sometimes complained of the "Calvinist-Copernican" system, indicating that they saw an unhappy parallel between reformed science and reformed religion.[18]

The Protestant Reformation also brought new approaches to the interpretation of scripture. Biblical texts had often been understood to carry several levels of meaning—symbolic and allegorical as well as literal. Disagreement between Catholics and Protestants over ultimate sources of authority, and the search for "proof texts" in disputes over doctrine, encouraged literal over symbolic readings. This change of emphasis when interpreting the book of God's word had consequences for the interpretation of God's other book, the book of his works. Nature ceased to be a deposit of unconnected religious symbols and became instead an ordered system, designed for human benefit, in which the connections between phenomena could be explored.[19] So we find Isaac Newton, who happened to be born on Christmas day, dedicating himself to a radical Christian mission having two parallel aims—to uncover single definitive meanings of each biblical text, just as he searched for a single definitive explanation for each natural phenomenon. Newton prescribed set rules for the reading of the two books, drawing an explicit analogy between them in a quest for the simplest interpretations.[20] This "two books" analogy had already served Francis Bacon well when he argued that because it was the duty of the Christian to study the Bible, it was also a religious duty to study the book of nature.

This by no means exhausts the connections that were made between Protestant Christianity and the importance of scientific study. The biblical doctrine of the Fall of man featured prominently in Bacon's vision. Through disobedience Adam had lost the dominion over nature that God had intended for humankind. Bacon's thesis was that the practical application of scientific knowledge could go some way at least to restoring that lost dominion.[21] Among the intellectual leaders of the puritan revolution in seventeenth-century England, another Christian motif helped to motivate a search for knowledge that would bring glory to God and relief to suffering humanity. This was the doctrine of Christ's second coming, when, on one reading of scripture, he would reign over the Earth for one thousand years. Bacon argued that to improve the world through the application of science was an appropriate way to prepare for the millennium. The Western dream of a science-based utopia owes much to the secularization of that millenarian vision.[22]

Conflict between Catholic and Protestant Christianity had some negative consequences for scientific innovation. Galileo suffered because his defense of a moving Earth coincided with attempts by the Catholic Church in Rome to reassert its authority during the Counter-Reformation. By the early 1630s Pope Urban VIII, who before he became pope had shown respect for Galileo, was under pressure from Spain, where he was criticized for being too lenient with heretics. When, in his book on the Copernican system, Galileo disobeyed Urban's instructions, it was easy to see this as a betrayal of trust. By ascribing tidal phenomena to a combination of the Earth's motions (axial rotation and revolution around the sun), Galileo marginalized Urban's philosophical thesis that scientific theorizing must always reckon with the fact that an omnipotent deity could have devised any number of mechanisms to produce a particular effect. Galileo was duly punished, but in circumstances that have haunted the Roman Church ever since. Unwisely, the scientific question of whether the Earth moved or not was translated into a question of faith, with tragic consequences.[23]

The combination of the Galileo story with evidence for a Protestant stimulus to science can easily give the impression that the Catholic Church was generally hostile to scientific innovation. This impression would be false on at least three counts. First, the Church had played a crucial role in the patronage of the sciences. The distinguished historian of science John Heilbron writes that "the Roman Catholic Church gave more financial and social support to the study of astronomy for over six centuries, from the recovery of ancient learning during the late Middle Ages into the Enlightenment, than any other, and, probably, all other, institutions."[24] Second, the Jesuit order within the Church contained outstanding astronomers, mathematicians, and physicists who were also committed to teaching the sciences in their educational programs.[25] Third, some of the greatest and most influential scientists of the seventeenth century were Catholics. Galileo, Mersenne, Gassendi, and Descartes all played prominent roles in the mechanization of nature.[26]

Instead of comparing the world to a living organism, Descartes saw nature as a complex piece of machinery. It was like the great cathedral clock in Strasbourg. In this mechanical philosophy, as it became known, the aim of science was to discover the invisible mechanisms that lay behind natural phenomena. In many respects it was a program that continues to this day. Descartes did not reduce the human mind (and the soul) to material processes, but everything else in nature was to be explained by the arrangement and motion of particles. This new way of looking at nature owed a lot to the recovery of ancient atomic theories of matter that were associated with Epicurus and Lucretius. And *there* was the problem: atomism in the ancient world had been associated with atheism. If the universe was simply the product of a chance collision of atoms, what room was there for a loving and merciful God?

This was the challenge that Christian natural philosophers had to take up if they were not to be accused of atheism themselves. Their response was to turn the argument around. How could the random motion of particles possibly produce the wonderfully organized world around us?[27] What about the human eye? Was it not obviously designed for the purpose of seeing? And if the physical world really were like the great clock at Strasbourg, would that not be proof of a designer? Clocks cannot assemble themselves! That was how Robert Boyle argued in his fusion of mechanism with providence. Boyle was not an ordained clergyman in the Christian church. But as an orthodox Christian, he described himself as a "priest in the temple of nature."[28] His use of the clock analogy did generate some problems of its own. There was a risk that the Creator might be seen as nothing more than a clockmaker, a very different image from the God who had redeemed the word through the death and resurrection of Jesus Christ. If the world is like a clock, there is also the question whether, once made, it can run by itself. Or might it need winding up from time to time? Newton collided with Leibniz on this particular point. When Newton suggested that the solar system needed an occasional readjustment to keep the planets in their orbits, Leibniz accused him of turning God into a second-rate clockmaker.[29] Despite their drawbacks, clockwork analogies featured prominently in works of Christian natural theology until well into the nineteenth century. Arguments for design in nature helped to make Christianity reasonable and science politically safe.[30]

Before moving into the Enlightenment and forward to the nineteenth century, two points deserve special emphasis. It is often said that during the scientific revolution of the seventeenth century, science became separated from religion. This is a vague proposition; the reality was very different.[31] As we have just seen, new ways were found for integrating scientific initiatives with belief in a wise and powerful Creator. There may have been separation on some levels, but on others there was an "unprecedented fusion."[32] Newton, for example, understood space to be constituted by God's omnipresence. He also understood the laws of nature to be universal because they originated in and were sustained by one God.[33] Second, there is no doubt that the Christian religion could, and did, provide intellectual resources for the support and justification of scientific activity. The various connections I have mentioned helped to make the sciences socially respectable when the dream of power over nature still had connotations of magic, greed, and irreligion. To say that without Christianity there would have been no modern science is to exaggerate. But it is not a myth that the reformulation of Christian doctrines played a crucial role in ensuring that an emerging scientific movement would become an enduring scientific culture.[34]

The eighteenth-century Enlightenment took different forms in different European countries. In France, for example, Voltaire welcomed Newton's science as a vehicle for exposing the superstition that he saw in the teachings of an intolerant church. By contrast, in England a Newtonian natural theology helped to preserve a sense of harmony between science and a religious sensibility.[35] For social reformers, scientific progress became both a *model for* and a *means to* social progress. So, still in England, we find a strong correlation between dissenting forms of Christianity and enthusiasm for science.[36] The evangelical preacher John Wesley was particularly anxious that the poor in society should have the benefit of the best medical advice, and he wrote a popular medical text that he kept revising to meet that need.[37] A very different example would be the dissenting minister Joseph Priestley, a name that may be familiar as one of the discoverers of oxygen. Priestley was deeply committed to science and to his own brand of Christianity because he believed that they were fighting on the same side against popular superstition. His theology was radical because he rejected the doctrine of the Trinity, seeing himself as defending a primitive, purified Christianity from the attacks of French atheists. He had once met some of them on a visit to France. He had been dining at the table of M. Turgot and was told by M. de Chattelux, he recalled, that "the two gentlemen opposite me were the Bishop of Aix and the Archbishop of Toulouse 'but,' said he, 'they are no more believers than you or I.' I assured him that I was a believer; but he would not believe me."[38]

Science was occasionally linked to materialism and atheism in eighteenth-century France. In the 1740s sensational experimental discoveries were enlisted to support the view that matter needed no help from spirits or gods. It could organize itself. Notable among these was the discovery by Abraham Trembley that a freshwater polyp, the hydra, after being chopped to pieces, could regenerate itself.[39] So sensational was the news that a wave of polyp-chopping swept across Europe. More seriously, by the end of the eighteenth century, Christians had to come to terms with the fact that scientific advances were beginning to correct traditional understandings of what was meant by "the creation" that God had made. The age of the Earth had to be expanded; more important, the Earth acquired a new history. Whereas a prominent Christian naturalist of the late seventeenth century, John Ray, had supposed that the creation had not significantly changed over time, a more complex and sometimes disturbing vista was opening up.[40] The traditional assumption was that human beings had been on Earth from the beginning. Evidence quickly mounted to support the speculation of the French naturalist Georges Buffon that the human race had appeared very late in time. Another Frenchman, Pierre-Simon Laplace, offered an account of the origins of the solar system without Newtonian references to a Creator.[41] Yet another Frenchman, Jean-Baptiste Lamarck, speculated that humans had developed from lower animals in the great chain of being, an inner drive to greater complexity propelling the transformation.[42] These could be troubling disclosures and were made more so in the early years of the nineteenth century when geologists realized, from the fossil record, just how many of God's creatures had become extinct.[43] If Christianity had once nurtured the sciences, by the early years of the nineteenth century it could easily look as if the sciences were now in rebellion. The climax to these developments in the historical sciences was, of course, Charles Darwin's theory of evolution by natural selection, published in his *On the Origin of Species* (1859).

The history of Darwinism within Christendom is a rich and complex subject. Countless books have been written on the topic, many vitiated by their aggressive agendas whether for Darwin or against. Looking at the contest today between vociferous Darwinian atheists on the one side and either young-earth creationists or advocates of intelligent design on the other, it would be easy to imagine that there have been no mediators. Darwinism has certainly been a divisive force within Christendom, but it has not been as destructive as many of its antireligious advocates have wished.[44] Darwin himself became an agnostic, but he stated clearly that it would be absurd to suppose that an ardent theist could not also be an evolutionist. One of his earliest converts was Charles Kingsley, a Christian clergyman. For Kingsley, a God who could make things *make themselves* was more to be admired than one who had simply made things.[45]

There has assuredly been a tradition of Christian resistance both to the idea of our animal ancestry and to the specific mechanism of natural selection.[46] Even some of Darwin's closest scientific allies, such as Charles Lyell (a crypto-Unitarian) and Alfred Russel Wallace (who would veer into spiritualism), doubted that natural selection could offer a sufficient account of the emergence of mind.[47] When the bishop of Oxford, Samuel Wilberforce, launched a public attack on Darwin's theory in 1860, he simply could not accept that human beings, for whom Jesus Christ had lived and died, shared a common ancestor with the apes. And yet, coinciding with that same Oxford meeting of the British Association, a future Archbishop of Canterbury, Frederick Temple, preached a sermon in which he welcomed the expansion of naturalistic explanation. The greater the number of phenomena brought under the reign of physical law, Temple argued, the stronger the case for asserting, by analogy, the existence of moral laws to which humans were subject.[48]

Darwin's leading advocate in North America was Harvard botanist Asa Gray, a committed Presbyterian Christian. Gray recognized that Darwin's theory was likely to offend religious sensibilities. The image of a perpetual war in nature, of fierce competition for limited resources, of repeated branching and further diversification in a nonlinear trajectory of species transformation, added to existing concerns about the loss of human dignity. Is this how an omnipotent, merciful God would arrange for increasingly complex life forms to develop? But perhaps, Gray suggested, pain and suffering could be better understood if they were seen as preconditions of the very possibility of human evolution.[49] Gray shared with Temple the conviction that Darwin's theory offered a more unified understanding of God's role in creation than traditional models in which every species was the result of a separate creative act. For Gray, for Wallace, and for Darwin himself, this unification justified belief in the unity of humankind. Their targets were those who proposed multiple origins for different human races, especially those who used that polygenism to justify slavery.[50]

That particular debate took place long ago, but it serves as a reminder that discussions about the relations between Christianity and science take place in specific locations and in specific political contexts.[51] Of course, many issues recur in those discussions. Are all events in nature under the immediate control of

God or, if not, to what degree does nature have its own autonomy? How are concepts of the miraculous to be explicated? How far are human freedoms and responsibilities threatened by mechanistic, deterministic accounts of the brain's operations? In twentieth-century debates fresh input from the physical and human sciences helped to keep scientific and theological discourse in contact despite many pressures for their severance.[52] What bearing if any does the indeterminacy disclosed by quantum mechanics have on our understanding of causality and the possible openness of the world to a providential deity? How wisely can the so-called anthropic coincidences (the apparent fine-tuning of physical parameters and constants for the eventual emergence of human life) be invoked to revitalize deflated arguments for design? Do Christian beliefs and values still have a role to play in shaping priorities for scientific research and its applications? And, given the ideological exploitation of science by enemies of the Christian faith, what qualifications are there to claims that scientific theories entail adverse consequences for theology, or that the intrinsic secularity of modern scientific culture has an inexorably corrosive effect on older wisdoms and spiritualities? These are just some of the questions that have invited deeper reflection in current literature on science and religion.[53]

Notes

1. Particularly influential in sustaining a conflict narrative were two late-nineteenth-century works: John W. Draper, *History of the Conflict between Religion and Science* (London: Henry S. King & Co., 1875); and Andrew Dickson White, *A History of the Warfare of Science with Theology in Christendom*, 2 vols. (New York: D. Appleton & Co., 1896). For a recent commentary on the conflict model, see Geoffrey Cantor, "What Shall We Do with the 'Conflict Thesis'?," in *Science and Religion: New Historical Perspectives*, ed. Thomas Dixon, Geoffrey Cantor, and Stephen Pumfrey (Cambridge: Cambridge University Press, 2010), 283–96.

2. Examples here include Stanley L. Jaki, *The Road of Science and the Ways to God* (Chicago: University of Chicago Press, 1978); and Rodney Stark, *For the Glory of God: How Monotheism Led to Reformations, Science, Witch-hunts and the End of Slavery* (Princeton, NJ: Princeton University Press, 2003).

3. Letter of Isaac Newton to Richard Bentley, in *Newton's Philosophy of Nature*, ed. H. S. Thayer (New York: Hafner, 1953), 48–49. See also Frank Manuel, *The Religion of Isaac Newton* (Oxford: Oxford University Press, 1974); and Stephen D. Snobelen, "'God of Gods, and Lord of Lords': The Theology of Isaac Newton's General Scholium to the *Principia*," *Osiris* 16 (2001): 169–208.

4. Ahmad S. Dallal, "Early Islam," in *Science and Religion around the World*, ed. John Hedley Brooke and Ronald L. Numbers (New York: Oxford University Press, 2011), 120–47; and

Ahmad S. Dallal, *Islam, Science, and the Challenge of History* (New Haven, CT: Yale University Press, 2010).

5. Noah Efron, "[The Myth] That Christianity Gave Birth to Modern Science," in *Galileo Goes to Jail and Other Myths about Science and Religion*, ed. Ronald L. Numbers (Cambridge, MA: Harvard University Press, 2009), 79–89.

6. John Hedley Brooke, *Science and Religion: Some Historical Perspectives* (Cambridge: Cambridge University Press, 1991).

7. Tertullian's "On Prescription against Heretics," quoted in David C. Lindberg, "Science and the Early Church," in *God and Nature: Historical Essays on the Encounter between Christianity and Science*, ed. David C. Lindberg and Ronald L. Numbers (Berkeley: University of California Press, 1986), 19–48, at 25.

8. Lindberg, "Science and the Early Church," 34.

9. J. H. Taylor, *Ancient Christian Writers*, 2 vols. (New York: Newman Press, 1982), 1:179.

10. For the long-term importance and influence of Augustine's position, see Ernan McMullin, "Darwin and the Other Christian Tradition," *Zygon* 46, no. 2 (2011): 291–316.

11. David C. Lindberg, "The Medieval Church Encounters the Classical Tradition: Saint Augustine, Roger Bacon, and the Handmaiden Metaphor," in *When Science and Christianity Meet*, ed. David C. Lindberg and Ronald L. Numbers (Chicago: University of Chicago Press, 2003), 7–32, at 15.

12. Peter Harrison and David C. Lindberg, "Early Christianity," in *Science and Religion around the World*, ed. John Hedley Brooke and Ronald L. Numbers (New York: Oxford University Press, 2011), 67–91, especially 73–75.

13. Robert Lenoble, *Mersenne ou la naissance du mécanisme* (Paris: J. Vrin, 1971).

14. The justification of empirical methods in the sciences through appeals to the primacy of God's free agency is a correlation that has attracted a significant body of scholarship, critically reviewed by Peter Harrison, "Voluntarism and Early Modern Science," *History of Science* 40 (2002): 63–89.

15. J. Y. Simpson, *Landmarks in the Struggle between Science and Religion* (London: Hodder and Stoughton, 1925), 139–40.

16. Harrison and Lindberg, "Early Christianity," 81.

17. Peter Barker, "The Lutheran Contribution to the Astronomical Revolution: Science and Religion in the Sixteenth Century," in *Religious Values and the Rise of Science in Europe*, ed. John Brooke and Ekmeleddin Ihsanoğlu (Istanbul: IRCICA, 2005), 31–62; and Kenneth J. Howell, *God's Two Books: Copernican Cosmology and Biblical Interpretation in Early Modern Science* (Notre Dame: University of Notre Dame Press, 2002), 109–35.

18. Howell, *God's Two Books*, 154–60.

19. Peter Harrison, *The Bible, Protestantism and the Rise of Natural Science* (Cambridge: Cambridge University Press, 1998).

20. Newton's hermeneutic rules can be found in Manuel, *The Religion of Isaac Newton*, 116–19.

21. Peter Harrison, *The Fall of Man and the Foundations of Science* (Cambridge: Cambridge University Press, 2007).

22. Charles Webster, *The Great Instauration: Science, Medicine, and Reform, 1626–1660* (London: Duckworth, 1975); and E. L. Tuveson, *Millennium and Utopia* (New York: Harper, 1964).

23. Ernan McMullin, ed., *The Church and Galileo* (Notre Dame, IN: University of Notre Dame Press, 2005); and Maurice A. Finocchiaro, *Retrying Galileo, 1633–1992* (Berkeley: University of California Press, 2005).

24. J. L. Heilbron, *The Sun in the Church: Cathedrals as Solar Observatories* (Cambridge MA: Harvard University Press, 1999), 3.

25. Ibid., 188–94.

26. Brooke, *Science and Religion*, 116–51; William B. Ashworth Jr., "Catholicism and Early Modern Science," in *God and Nature: Historical Essays on the Encounter between Christianity and Science*, ed. David C. Lindberg and Ronald L. Numbers (Berkeley: University of California Press, 1986), 136–66; and Lawrence M. Principe, "[The Myth] That Catholics Did Not Contribute to the Scientific Revolution," in *Galileo Goes to Jail and Other Myths about Science and Religion*, ed. Ronald L. Numbers (Cambridge, MA: Harvard University Press, 2009), 99–106.

27. Margaret J. Osler, *Reconfiguring the World: Nature, God, and Human Understanding from the Middle Ages to Early Modern Europe* (Baltimore: Johns Hopkins University Press, 2010), 77–93.

28. Michael Hunter, *Between God and Science* (New Haven, CT: Yale University Press, 2009); and R. Hooykaas, *Robert Boyle: A Study in Science and Christian Belief*, with a foreword by John Hedley Brooke and Michael Hunter (Lanham, MD: University Press of America, 1997).

29. H. G. Alexander, ed., *The Leibniz-Clarke Correspondence* (Manchester: Manchester University Press, 1956).

30. John Brooke and Geoffrey Cantor, *Reconstructing Nature: The Engagement of Science and Religion* (Edinburgh: T & T Clark, 1998), 141–243. For English natural theology in the first half of the nineteenth century, see Jonathan R. Topham, "Biology in the Service of Natural Theology: Paley, Darwin and the *Bridgewater Treatises*," in *Biology and Ideology: From Descartes to Dawkins*, ed. Denis R. Alexander and Ronald L. Numbers (Chicago: University of Chicago Press, 2010), 88–113.

31. Margaret J. Osler, "[The Myth] That the Scientific Revolution Liberated Science from Religion," in *Galileo Goes to Jail and Other Myths about Science and Religion*, ed. Ronald L. Numbers (Cambridge, MA: Harvard University Press, 2009), 90–98; and Brooke, *Science and Religion*, 52–81.

32. Amos Funkenstein, *Theology and the Scientific Imagination from the Middle Ages to the Seventeenth Century* (Princeton, NJ: Princeton University Press, 1986), 89–97.

33. Stephen D. Snobelen, "'The True Frame of Nature': Isaac Newton, Heresy, and the Reformation of Natural Philosophy," in *Heterodoxy in Early Modern Science and Religion*, ed. John Brooke and Ian Maclean (Oxford: Oxford University Press, 2005), 223–62, especially 253.

34. Stephen Gaukroger, *The Emergence of a Scientific Culture: Science and the Shaping of Modernity* (Oxford: Clarendon Press, 2006).

35. John Gascoigne, "From Bentley to the Victorians: The Rise and Fall of British Newtonian Natural Theology," *Science in Context* 2 (1988): 219–56.

36. Paul Wood, ed., *Science and Dissent in England, 1688–1945* (Aldershot, UK: Ashgate, 2004).

37. Deborah Madden, *"A Cheap, Safe and Natural Medicine": Religion, Medicine and Culture in John Wesley's Primitive Physic*, Wellcome Series in the History of Medicine (Amsterdam: Editions Rodopi, 2007).

38. Quoted in A. D. Orange, "Oxygen and One God: Joseph Priestley in 1774," *History Today* 24 (1974): 773; and John Brooke, "Joining Natural Philosophy to Christianity: The Case of Joseph Priestley," in *Heterodoxy in Early Modern Science and Religion*, ed. John Brooke and Ian Maclean (Oxford: Oxford University Press, 2005), 319–36.

39. Brooke, *Science and Religion*, 171–80.

40. Martin J. S. Rudwick, *Bursting the Limits of Time: The Reconstruction of Geohistory in the Age of Revolution* (Chicago: University of Chicago Press, 2005).

41. For the religious implications of Laplace's "nebular hypothesis," see Ronald L. Numbers, *Creation by Natural Law: Laplace's Nebular Hypothesis in American Thought* (Seattle: University of Washington Press, 1977).

42. Ludmilla Jordanova, "Nature's Powers: A Reading of Lamarck's Distinction between Creation and Production," in *History, Humanity and Evolution*, ed. James R. Moore (Cambridge: University of Cambridge Press, 1989), 71–98.

43. Rudwick, *Bursting the Limits of Time*, 505–12.

44. For a sophisticated theological diagnosis of the intellectual myopia present in today's warring factions, see Conor Cunningham, *Darwin's Pious Idea: Why the Ultra-Darwinists and Creationists Get It Wrong* (Grand Rapids, MI: Eerdmans, 2010), 377–412.

45. References to Darwin's own views on religion and to the immediate reactions of others to his science can be found elsewhere in this book in the section devoted specifically to Darwin.

46. Frederick Gregory, "The Impact of Darwinian Evolution on Protestant Theology in the Nineteenth Century," in *God and Nature: Historical Essays on the Encounter between Christianity and Science*, ed. David C. Lindberg and Ronald L. Numbers (Berkeley: University of California Press, 1986), 369–90; and Mariano Artigas, Thomas F. Glick, and Rafael A. Martinez, ed., *Negotiating Darwin: The Vatican Confronts Evolution 1877–1902* (Baltimore: Johns Hopkins University Press, 2006).

47. Peter J. Bowler, *Charles Darwin: The Man and His Influence* (Oxford: Blackwell, 1990), 177–201.

48. Frederick Temple, *The Present Relations of Science to Religion* (Oxford: Parker, 1860).

49. Asa Gray, *Darwiniana*, ed. A. Hunter Dupree (Cambridge MA: Harvard University Press, 1963), 310–11. For a recent Christian articulation of a similar argument, see Christopher Southgate, *The Groaning of Creation: God, Evolution, and the Problem of Evil* (Louisville, KY: Westminster John Knox Press, 2008). Southgate writes: "Since this was the world the God of all creativity and all compassion chose for the creation of creatures, we must presume that this was the only type of world that would do for that process" (90).

50. Adrian Desmond and James Moore, *Darwin's Sacred Cause: Race, Slavery and the Quest for Human Origins* (London: Allen Lane, 2009).

51. David N. Livingstone, "Re-placing Darwinism and Christianity," in *When Science and Christianity Meet*, ed. David C. Lindberg and Ronald L. Numbers (Chicago: University of Chicago Press, 2003), 183–202; and David N. Livingstone, *Putting Science in Its Place: Geographies of Scientific Knowledge* (Chicago: University of Chicago Press, 2003).

52. John Hedley Brooke, "Modern Christianity," in *Science and Religion around the World*, ed. John Hedley Brooke and Ronald L. Numbers (New York: Oxford University Press, 2011), 111–14.

53. For guidance on the state of such debates, see Keith Ward, *The Big Questions in Science and Religion* (West Conshohocken, PA: Templeton Foundation Press, 2008); Peter Harrison, ed., *The Cambridge Companion to Science and Religion* (Cambridge: Cambridge University Press, 2010); and Philip Clayton, ed., *The Oxford Handbook of Religion and Science* (Oxford: Oxford University Press, 2006).

Science and Religion in the History of Islam

AHMAD DALLAL

BEFORE THE COMING OF ISLAM, and for over a century after its rise, Arabs had no science. Without exception, historians of Islamic science have rightly identified the "translation movement," the bulk of which took place in the course of the ninth century, as the most important factor in the emergence of an Islamic scientific culture. This translation movement provided the knowledge base of the emergent sciences. However, the scientific activity that followed was a complex phenomenon that does not lend itself to single track and static explanations and is not reducible to translation. Despite the paramount importance of the Greek scientific tradition, Arabic science was not a mere museum of Greek scientific knowledge. Evidence from the earliest extant scientific sources indicates that the translation movement was concurrent with, rather than a prerequisite for, scientific research in the Islamic world. Simultaneous research and translation took place in more than one field, and in more than one case, even when some of the scientific texts were being translated, they were also reformulated and transformed. As such, the translation movement itself was an aspect of an emerging scientific culture and not its mechanical cause. The practical social and political needs of vibrant Muslim societies and polities, coupled with theoretical and scholarly needs, gave rise to and nurtured a systematic translation movement that had a great impact on the subsequent development of a scientific culture in the Muslim world.

Beyond beginnings, however, the scale of Islamic scientific activities is vast. Science in medieval Muslim societies was practiced on a scale unprecedented in earlier or contemporary human history. In urban centers from the Atlantic to the borders of China, thousands of scientists pursued careers in diverse scientific disciplines that far exceeded the number of sciences practiced in antiquity. Until the rise of modern science, no other civilization engaged as many scientists, produced as many scientific books, or provided as varied and sustained support for scientific activity.

Historical and literary sources of various kinds provide abundant evidence for the social respectability of many branches of the rational sciences such as logic, arithmetic, medicine, geometry, astronomy, algebra, and philosophy. For example, the biographical dictionaries of religious scholars often celebrate their knowledge of the rational sciences. Many of these scholars combined expertise in the religious and rational sciences. Furthermore, specialized biographical dictionaries were compiled to celebrate scientists; biographical dictionaries, it should be noted, serve the important function of identifying and sanctioning communities of scholars. Another indicator of the respectability of rational sciences is the use of the same discourse and idioms in praising knowledge in rational as well as religious sciences. Finally, the constant presence of the rational sciences in all classification of sciences reflects not just social but also epistemological sanction of the rational sciences.

Historical sources indicate that the twelfth and thirteenth centuries witnessed a shifting professional alliance between various religious and rational disciplines, providing new space for the intersection of rational and religious sciences, thereby lending the rational sciences added prestige and respectability. For example, as of the twelfth century, a large number of scholars specialized in ḥadīth (traditions of the Prophet Muḥammad) and medicine, including the famous thirteenth-century scholar Ibn al-Nafīs who discovered the pulmonary circulation of blood. Another common specialization in this period combines the subjects of *uṣūl al-dīn* (principles of religion), *uṣūl al-fiqh* (principles of jurisprudence), and logic; or theology (*kalām*), logic, and astronomy. Further evidence suggests that scientific education was pervasive and widespread through at least the sixteenth century and was central to mainstream intellectual life in Muslim societies. This integration is reflected in the large number of religious scholars who were also competent and original scientists.

In addition to the combination of specific scientific and religious disciplines in the persons of individual scholars, several scientific subfields were integrated into the standard curriculum of religious educational institutions. These include the fields of *farā'iḍ* (inheritance algebra), a subfield of algebra that deals with inheritance law, and *'ilm al-mīqāt* (time keeping), a subfield of practical astronomy that deals with such questions as timekeeping, finding the direction of prayer, and lunar visibility computations.

In addition to enhancing the status of the mother disciplines, the integration of the subfields of astronomy and mathematics into religious education also provided institutional support to these disciplines. So, for example, beginning at least in the twelfth century, the office of a timekeeper (*muwaqqit*) was established in most major mosques to solve problems of mathematical astronomy emerging from an Islamic cultural context, such as finding the direction of qibla, times of prayer, and lunar visibility. Astronomers occupying this office attended to these practical needs, but in their spare time they also pursued research agendas having nothing to do with these practical needs. Some of the most original research in planetary theory was done by timekeepers, including the famous work of the fourteenth-century Damascene astronomer Ibn al-Shāṭir.

Contrary to initial impressions, however, the integration of these subfields of science into the curriculum of religious education did not undermine the autonomy of these fields. Rather, this integration of the subfields of astronomy and mathematics enhanced the standing of these sciences in general without inhibiting the pursuit of other branches of these sciences that were not integrated into the religious curriculum.

But how are we to characterize the relationship between science and religion in light of the actual history of the Islamic sciences? To answer this question, I focus on one particular example of great significance before venturing some general conclusions.[1] This is the example of the qibla. During their five daily prayers, Muslims are required to face Mecca, and all mosques are supposed to be oriented toward the Ka'ba in Mecca, or what is known as the direction of the qibla. Before the availability of mathematical methods, Muslims followed the practices of the early Companions of the Prophet Muhammad and their successors to determine the direction of the qibla. They also made use of traditions of folk astronomy and of the fact that the Ka'ba is itself astronomically aligned. These methods provided reasonable approximations in locations close to Mecca, but further away, in places like North Africa and Iran, they were quite inaccurate. With the emergence of mathematical sciences, new mathematical methods of considerable sophistication were devised to compute the qibla for any locality on the basis of the geographical coordinates of that locality and of Mecca. Finding the direction of the qibla was a favorite problem for medieval astronomers, and it was treated in separate works, in sections of astronomical handbooks, or in manuals for timekeeping. Some of the greatest minds among the Muslim astronomers turned their attention to this problem and devised for this purpose solutions of considerable sophistication. The development of methods reflected a development in the use of mathematical techniques: the earliest and least complex methods were approximations; next, solid geometry was used to accurately calculate the direction of the qibla; various analemmas were then employed to solve the problem of the qibla graphically; finally, using spherical trigonometry, specifically the theorem of Menelaos or the simpler sine theorem, the direction of the qibla could be derived by using entities on the surface of the sphere. Moreover, numerous tables giving the direction of the qibla for different localities were computed on the bases of each of these methods.

Beyond the Hijaz, Syria, and Iraq, many mosques built in the early period of Islamic expansion were misaligned. As knowledge of mathematical astronomy increased, this flaw was recognized, and while some of the misaligned mosques retained their orientation, others were rebuilt to face the qibla. However, to tear down mosques built on the authority of the Companions of the Prophet on the basis of the findings of mathematical astronomy presented a serious problem. More generally, the question was asked: Should mathematical knowledge take precedence over religious authority in a matter where, admittedly, the realms of science and religion overlapped?

The question of the qibla was discussed by many astronomers and religious scholars. One scholarly tradition of such discussions focuses on the misaligned mosques of Fes and includes writings from the twelfth through the end of the seventeenth centuries. The primary question addressed in these writings is whether the qibla is to be determined on the basis of religious precedence or mathematical astronomy.

One sixteenth-century religious scholar and timekeeper, al-Tājūrī, wrote a book on the problem of the qibla in which he solicits the fatwas (religious rulings) of the scholars of Cairo and Egypt about the mosques of Fes that were directed toward the south, including the city's famous al-Qarawiyyīn mosque, the most important mosque school complex in Morocco. Fes, it should be noted, is one of the most important cities in Morocco, and for much of the history of Islam in North Africa it was the political capital of the country as well as its scholarly capital. Moreover, in terms of Islamic education, al-Qarawiyyīn is the Moroccan equivalent of the Azhar University in Egypt.

Some Fasi scholars criticized al-Tājūrī, and a late-seventeenth-century scholar, Al-'Arabī Ibn 'Abd al-Salām al-Fāsī, came to his defense. Al-Fāsī refers to a distinction made by some scholars between the *jiha* of the qibla, which means the general direction, and the *samt* of the qibla, which means the precise azimuth of the zenith of Mecca. Those who make this distinction suggest that the law requires of Muslims only that they face the general direction of the qibla without requiring knowledge of its exact mathematical coordinates, which would involve knowledge of the science of geometry. These scholars argue that because there is no legal obligation to have knowledge of geometry, then no other legal obligations can be contingent on it. In response, al-Fāsī insists that the meanings of *jiha* and *samt* are the same, and that geometry is not different from any other commonly used skill such as construction and commerce "because each craft which involves precision and measurement partakes in geometry. In fact, it is even possible to chastise a person capable of finding the exact direction of Mecca who leaves that and instead imitates the niche (miḥrāb)" which is erected in the interest of people who have no knowledge of the ways of finding the direction of the qibla.[2] Al-Fāsī next distinguishes between two senses of the term *jiha* (direction): as an objective in itself (*maqṣad*) or as a means (*wasīla*) for finding the direction. The ultimate objective, he adds, is to find the mathematical coordinates of the direction of the Ka'ba. Furthermore, "the exercise of independent legal reasoning (*ijtihād*) in matters related to the qibla is only valid through use of proofs which are suitable for finding this direction and not through guess and conjecture."[3] Al-Fāsī then refers to a fatwa attributed to Imām Mālik—whose doctrine is the official legal school of North Africa—that if the orientation of a mosque is based on *ijtihād*, then an error does not require rebuilding it. In response al-Fāsī maintains that although this would be true if the *ijtihād* is based on proofs derived from astronomy or from the use of astronomical tables or the like, an *ijtihād* that is not based on proofs cannot be accepted.

After noting the argument that holding all Muslims responsible on the basis of mathematical knowledge that only a few can attain is contrary to the spirit of Islamic law, al-Fāsī retorts that:

> Each craft has its masters, and nothing comes easy; learning [how to find] the direction of the qibla is similar to learning other sciences; in fact, it might

even be easier than learning more elaborate texts, and it is attainable in a short period. In large cities, it is illegal for someone who does not know [how to find] the direction of the qibla to build a mosque, unless he is accompanied by masters of the craft who know the proofs of the qibla. It is only permissible to erect [a mosque which is oriented towards] the direction of Mecca, and someone who does not know the proofs of the qibla should not exercise his *ijtihād* even if he happens to be a jurist, *because the most a jurist can know in his capacity as a jurist is that it is obligatory to face the qibla, and that it is obligatory for a non-*mujtahid *to imitate a* mujtahid *in this matter, that is, to imitate one who knows the suitable proofs for it.*[4]

Elsewhere, al-Fāsī adds that:

> The real mujtahids in the matter of the qibla, using proofs suitable for it, are the astronomers, not the jurists. Because . . . the prerequisite of this [*ijtihād*] is knowledge derived from the sciences of mathematics, mathematical astronomy, timekeeping, the positions of the planets, and the computation of directions, and all of these are outside the domain of the legal science. . . . Furthermore, the *ijtihād* of astronomers in the matter of the qibla is not similar to the *ijtihād* of jurists in applied law, because there is only one correct outcome for the *ijtihād* in the qibla, whereas for jurists each *mujtahid* is correct in applied law. . . . This is why in the matter of the qibla the astronomers are given precedence over the jurists, because each craft has its masters, and the masters of the craft of [finding the direction of] the qibla are the astronomers.[5]

In the further stages of his treatise, al-Fāsī quotes and comments on numerous legal rulings and questions only to reiterate that "the *ijtihād* of the Companions [of the Prophet] is certain, that of jurists is probable and uncertain, and that of the astronomers in the [matter of the] qibla is scientific and technical which is equivalent to certainty, because they [the astronomers] and not the jurists know the proofs of the qibla. For these reasons, astronomers take precedence over jurists."[6]

The epistemological questions raised in these debates reflect widespread discussions taking place in many fields over a very long period of time. Owing to the practical nature of the qibla debate, the conceptual categories under discussion may at times appear vague, but these issues were articulated much more precisely in other theoretical debates. The significance of the qibla debate is that precise epistemological discussions filtered down to the most sensitive matter of prayer, raising in no uncertain terms the question of intellectual authority within Islam's most sacred space. Clearly, this was not an academic debate carried out on the margins of Islamic culture but rather a debate that is constitutive of this culture and a characteristic feature of it.

To generalize the conclusions that can be drawn from this important debate, let me briefly touch on three fields at the intersection of science and religion, as seen through the prism of three respective scholars. In his anthropological history of India, the eleventh-century astronomer Abū Rayḥān al-Bīrūnī (d. 1048), one of the most prolific scientists of his time and one of the greatest Muslim scientists of all times, starts a chapter, "On the Configuration of the Heavens and the Earth According to [Indian] Astrologers," with an extended comparison between the cultural imperatives of Muslim and Indian sciences. The views of Indian astrologers, Bīrūnī maintains, "have developed in a way which is different from those of our [Muslim] fellows; this is because, unlike the scriptures revealed before it, the Qur'ān does not articulate on this subject [of astronomy], or any other [field of] necessary [knowledge], any assertion that would require erratic interpretations in order to harmonize it with that which is known by necessity." The Qur'ān, he adds, does not address matters on which there is endless disagreement, such as history. Certainly, Islam has suffered from those who claimed to be Muslims while retaining many of the teachings of earlier religions and who claimed that these are part of the doctrines of Islam. Such, for example, were the Manichaeans, whose religious doctrine and mistaken views about the heavens were wrongly attributed to Islam. Such attributions of scientific views to the Qur'ān are, according to Bīrūnī, false claims of un-Islamic origins. In contrast, all the religious and transmitted books of the Indians do indeed speak "of the configuration of the universe in a way which contradicts the truth which is known to their own astrologers." However, driven by the need to uphold their religious traditions, Indian astrologers pretend to believe in the astrological doctrines of these books even when aware of their falsity. With the passage of time, accurate astronomical doctrines were mixed with those advanced in the religious books, which led to the confusion to be encountered in Indian astronomy.[7]

Although Bīrūnī recognizes that not all Indian religious views contradict the dictates of astronomy, he still maintains that the conflation of religious and astronomical knowledge undermines Indian astronomy and explains its errors and weaknesses. Bīrūnī compares this conflation of scripture and science with the Islamic astronomical tradition that, in his view, suffers from no such short-comings. In Bīrūnī's view, therefore, the Qur'ān and religious dogma do not interfere in the business of science, nor do they infringe on its realm. Evidence from the writings of religious scholars suggests that Bīrūnī's view was in conformity with prevalent views within Islamic discursive culture. This conflu-ence of attitudes between scientists such as Bīrūnī and religious scholars further suggests a conceptual separation of science and religion in the main-stream of classical Islamic culture.

Bīrūnī's attitude seems to intersect in some important ways with that of al-Ghazālī (d. 1111), one of the most celebrated Muslim religious thinkers of all times. Ghazālī is often considered an enemy of science and one of the main causes for its decline. However, a closer examination of Ghazālī's views reflects a much more nuanced religious attitude toward the sciences. Ghazālī is critical of the metaphysical part of philosophy that, he argues, may be in conflict with religion. In his *Incoherence of the Philosophers*, Ghazālī maintains that philosophers cannot claim harmony between their beliefs and the tenets of Islam.[8] Out of some twenty criticisms of philosophical assertions, Ghazālī's attack on philosophers revolves around three main points of contention with the Islamic Aristotelians: their assertion that the world is eternal; their denial of God's knowledge of particulars; and their denial of the resurrection of bodies. What Ghazālī objects to in philosophy is metaphysics, a science whose subject matter overlaps with that of theology. This is why, Ghazālī argues, religion is not silent on the implications of metaphysics. Furthermore, accord-ing to Ghazālī, philosophy as metaphysics fails to satisfy the conditions of demonstrative proof.

In contrast to his criticism of philosophy cum metaphysics, Ghazālī argues that mathematics is demonstrably true and has no bearing on religious matters. Ghazālī says that mathematicians ought to be warned against the educational package with which they are usually presented; that is, they should be warned against the possible philosophical underpinnings of their craft. However, this potential pitfall does not affect Ghazālī's positive evaluation of mathematical knowledge. Indeed, he goes out of his way to state that those who claim that religion is opposed to either mathematics or logic would be doing a great disservice to religion by posing it against something which cannot be refuted.

In his words, "such matters rest on geometrical and arithmetical demonstrations that leave no room for doubt. Thus when one who studies these demonstrations and ascertains their proofs . . . is told that this is contrary to religion, he will not suspect this science, but only religion."[9]

If mathematical knowledge is valid and undeniable, in Ghazālī's view, logic is a doctrinally neutral tool that is not just useful but also essential for all sciences, including theology, the science employed in the defense of religion, and the science of jurisprudence. Ghazālī's extensive discussion of logic not only legitimized logic from a religious point of view but also produced an Islamic discourse on the science of logic and replaced the technical terms used by earlier philosophers with terms used by jurists. As a result, the science of logic was naturalized and legitimized as an indispensable science for all forms of knowledge. In Ghazālī's words, logic is "no more than the study of the methods of proof and standards for reasoning, the conditions of the premises of demonstration and the manner of their ordering, the conditions of correct definition and the manner of its construction. . . . Nothing of this ought to be denied. It is the same kind of thing the theologians and religious speculative thinkers mention in their treatments of proof."[10]

Finally, Ghazālī maintains that a part of the natural sciences is demonstrable and certain. However, he rejects the principle of causation, which is the cornerstone of Aristotelian demonstrative science. Ghazālī resolves this apparent contradiction between the possibility of natural knowledge and the denial of causality by making a distinction between God's recurrent creation of the natural order and God's creation in humans of the knowledge of natural patterns. This distinction allows Ghazālī to argue that human knowledge of nature involves discerning uniformity in nature while denying that this uniformity is a natural necessity. In other words, natural causation is not necessary because actions belong to willing agents, and nature is not one. However, by shifting the discussion from the natural order to human knowledge of this order, Ghazālī maintains that scientists could study a habitual or customary natural order and at the same time accept the unlikely and statistically insignificant possibility of a disruption of this order, if or when the agent creating this order chooses to do so. If there is such a thing as a final definition of the orthodox position on science, it should be sought in the normative works that incontestably define orthodoxy and set its norms, and Ghazālī's works rank high among these. In fact, there is abundant evidence that the message of

Ghazālī was well received by other Muslims. The famous fourteenth-century historian Ibn Khaldūn mentions that, after Ghazālī, all religious scholars studied logic, but they studied it from new sources, and they stopped using the books of the ancients.[11]

Any discussion of the relation between science and religion in Islam must address the Qur'ānic attitude toward science.[12] The main source in which Qur'ānic paradigms of science are articulated is the genre of Qur'ānic exegesis (tafsīr). Rather than adducing a Qur'ānic stand on science by directly reading the Qur'ān, as many contemporary Muslims do, exegetical works represent a dynamic interaction between the scripture and the real historical communities that embodied Islamic culture. Although they insist on grounding themselves in the unchanging text of the Qur'ān, exegetical works are also repositories of larger cultural debates and reflect contemporary outlooks. Traditional Qur'ānic commentaries contain much material of possible scientific import. However, these traditional materials do not collectively add up to what might legitimately be regarded as a scientific interpretation of the Qur'ān. Their authors do not see themselves as engaging in such an interpretive exercise. Moreover, there are no instances in which exegetes claim authority in scientific subjects because of their knowledge of the Qur'ān.

The following examination of the treatment of scientific subjects in Qur'ānic exegesis is based primarily on the tafsīr of Fakhr al-Dīn al-Rāzī (d. 1210), one of the main representatives of the dominant theological school of Islam, the Ash'ari school, and perhaps the most distinguished member of this school after Ghazālī.[13] Rāzī wrote on natural philosophy and was fully familiar with the natural philosophical debates of the time. He also wrote an influential Qur'ānic exegesis that is notable for its discussions of quasi-scientific subjects; in fact, Rāzī's discussion of such subjects exceeds most other exegetical works of the classical period, and it certainly was more influential than any other exegesis of its genre.

The marvel of creation is a theme to be found frequently in Qur'ānic commentaries. These marvels are viewed as signs of God and proofs that he exists, is all-powerful and all-knowing, and is the willing Creator of all being. A much-quoted passage encouraging contemplation of the signs of the heavens and the earth is Qur'ān 3:190–91: "In the creation of the heavens and the earth, the alternation of night and day, are signs for the wise. Those who remember God, standing or sitting or lying on their sides, who reflect and contemplate on the creation of the heavens and the earth (and say): 'Not in vain have you made them. All praise be to you, O Lord preserve us from the torment of Hell.'" The most striking feature of the discussions of the Qur'ānic signs of creation, especially the heavenly ones, is the mixing of some information drawn from astronomy and natural philosophy with a wealth of other nonscientific information.

A further point made by the commentaries on the "sign verses" is that, although the complex perfection of creation is in itself a sign of the wise Creator, the primary proof is not just in the creation of this complex natural order but in the benefits that humanity derives from it. Commentaries thus typically focus on how various aspects of natural phenomena are arranged to maximize the benefits to humanity; because there is no inherent reason for the universe to be arranged in a particular fashion, it follows that there must be a maker who chose to create it as it is; the guiding principle is again human benefit. Thus, it is the benefit to humans that ultimately proves the existence of a wise and willing Creator.

Classical commentaries often include elaborate treatments of scientific subjects to illustrate the idea of God's wise choice of creation as a way of maximizing human benefit. Although the natural order is often discussed, it is the free volition of the maker and not any inherent nature that accounts for this order. It is evident that this elaborate, quasi-scientific discourse, drawing freely on the scientific knowledge of the time, does not seek to uphold a particular scientific view of nature. Moreover, it is equally true that this discourse does not seek to make positive contributions to the accepted body of scientific knowledge. Rather, its primary purpose is to argue that the created order is contingent and ultimately dependent on God. Nowhere does one encounter the notion that a certain scientific fact or theory is predicted or even favored by the Qur'ān. Instead, these commentaries reject interpretations of Qur'ānic verses grounded in the notion of a natural order. The sign verses serve as evidence of the Creator not because of the particular knowledge that they convey about nature but through the ultimate conclusion in every verse that there is a choice in creation and, thus, a Creator who makes this choice. In these commentaries scientific knowledge is freely invoked and occasionally challenged. Yet the purpose of rejecting some scientific views is not to promote alternative ones, nor to assert the authority of the Qur'ān at the expense of the various fields of science. In the absence of a clear statement in the Qur'ān, one seeks answers to scientific questions in their respective fields. The contrary, however, is not true because the text is not science. When there is an apparent conflict between a Qur'ānic text and a scientific fact, commentators do not present the Qur'ānic text as the arbiter but simply try to explore the possibility of alternative scientific explanations and thus suggest that scientific knowledge on such points of contention is not categorical.

Thus it follows that religious knowledge and scientific knowledge are each assigned to their own compartments. This would justify the pursuit of science and even the use of scientific discourse in commenting on the Qur'ān but would also limit this use. In classical *tafsīr* works, the Qur'ān does not have a scientific import and does not translate into binding scientific facts. It emphasizes the wisdom and power behind creation but says nothing about the exact order and workings of the created world. The complexity and wondrous nature of creation reinforce belief in God, but this is not contingent on the adoption of any particular scientific view. In fact, scientific facts and theories in themselves do not prove the oneness of the Creator. Rather, the very fact that other natural orders are possible points to a willing maker who chooses one of these possibilities. Thus everything in nature, however explained, as well as all scientific discoveries and facts irrespective of their certainty, serve as proofs for the existence of the maker. This is the fundamental reason why the scientific and unscientific could appear side by side in the commentaries on the Qur'ān.

A common trend runs through the religious formulations, the epistemological constructs, and the works of scientists. Philosophy, the overarching discipline in the Greek classifications of science, was gradually relegated in the Islamic hierarchy of knowledge to one subdivision among many other sciences. Having isolated philosophy, Muslims could then single it out as a potential source of conflict with religion without jeopardizing the other demonstrable sciences. Thus conceived, the areas in which science and religion overlap are reduced. As a result, one of the consequences of the Islamization of science in classical Muslim practice was the epistemological separation of science and philosophy, a separation that undermined the Aristotelian unity of knowledge and made possible the subsequent separation of religion and science.

Notes

1. The following section of this essay draws on my *Islam, Science, and the Challenge of History* (New Haven, CT: Yale University Press, 2010).

2. Al-'Arabī b 'Abd al-Salām al-Fāsī, *Shifā' al-ghalīl fī bayān qiblat ṣaḥib al-tanzīl*, al-Khizāna al-Ḥasaniyya (Royal Library), Rabat, ms. 6588, fol. 6.

3. Ibid., fol. 14.

4. Ibid., fols. 21–22. Emphasis added.

5. Ibid., fol. 32.

6. Ibid., fol. 81.

7. Abū Rayḥān Muḥammad ibn Aḥmad al-Bīrūnī, *Taḥqīq mā lil-Hind min maqūla ma'qūla fī al-'aql am mardhūla* (Beirut: 'Ālam al-Kitāb, n.d.), 219–21.

8. Abū Ḥāmid al-Ghazālī, *The Incoherence of the Philosophers/Tahāfut al-falāsifa, a Parallel English-Arabic Text*, ed. and trans. Michael Marmura (Provo, UT: Brigham Young University Press, 1997).

9. Abū Ḥāmid al-Ghazālī, *Tahāfut al-falāsifa*, ed. Sulaymān Dunyā (Cairo: Dār al-Ma'ārif, 1958), 78.

10. Abū Ḥāmid al-Ghazālī, *Al-Munqidh min al-ḍalāl*, ed. Jamīl Salība and Kāmil Ayyād (Beirut: Dār al-Andalus, 1983), 103–4.

11. Ibn Khaldūn, *The Muqaddimah*, trans. Franz Rosenthal, abridged by N. J. Dawood (Princeton, NJ: Princeton University Press, 1967), 143.

12. The following section of this essay draws on my article "Science and the Qur'ān" in Jane Dammen McAuliffe, ed., *Encyclopaedia of the Qur'ān* (Leiden: Brill, 2004), 4:540–58.

13. Fakhr al-Dīn al-Rāzī, *al-Tafsīr al-kabīr (Mafātīḥ al-ghayb)* (Beirut, 1981).

Science and Religious Belief in the Modern World

Challenges and Opportunities

DENIS ALEXANDER

IN 1968 THE LEADING AMERICAN SOCIOLOGIST Peter Berger wrote in the *New York Times*: "[By] the twenty-first century, religious believers are likely to be found only in small sects, huddled together to resist a worldwide secular culture."[1] But in 1999 the same Peter Berger wrote: "The assumption that we live in a secularized world is false. The world today, with some exceptions . . . , is as furiously religious as it ever was, and in some places more so than ever. This means that a whole body of literature by historians and social scientists loosely labeled 'secularization theory' is essentially mistaken."[2] Of course, much has happened since 1999 to support Berger's comment.

Indeed, one of the great surprises to many of my older secularized scientific colleagues in Britain has been the vigor of religion, not just as a private belief but also as an influence to be reckoned with out in the public domain. On the other hand, Western Europe in particular does remain a relatively secularized part of the world. And one characteristic of so-called post-Christian countries is the fragmentation of society into hundreds of cultural pieces. We have become pick-and-mix societies where people construct their worldviews from a huge range of options. This in turn makes the dialogue between science and religion much more complex.

Against this background of cultural fragmentation, I highlight three streams of thought in particular that represent challenges to the dialogue between science and religious belief in the modern world but at the same time provide some great opportunities: postmodernism; the so-called New Atheism; and fundamentalism. I review each one briefly in turn.

35

First, postmodernism. As a constructed body of ideas, postmodernism is clearly no longer such a feature of humanities departments in Western universities as it was a decade or so ago, though no doubt there are exceptions. Scientists have always been highly suspicious of postmodern ideas because, in its more extreme relativistic form, postmodernism can suggest that scientific knowledge is no more than one among many ways of looking at the physical reality of the world, all equally valid and culture-bound. By contrast, scientists would say that their models and data and discoveries are leading them onward to holding more truthful understandings of the world than they had before. It does not matter what your culture, language, or religion might be; DNA really is a double helix and not a triple helix anywhere in the world. The triple-helical model of DNA, which was indeed once suggested as its structure, is just wrong, and it is wrong for everybody.

If scientists then seek to engage postmodern forms of religion in which religion has been watered down to an existential faith or repackaged as a set of spiritual principles rather than presented as an evidence-based, rational faith that seeks to tell truths about the world, then a significant shared space for the dialogue between science and religion is lost. In this case the scientist can readily become frustrated with a set of ideas that seem to make no truth claims at all about the world.

It is interesting to note that at my own University at Cambridge there are far more active Christians in the science faculties than in the humanities faculties. In fact, the proportion of active Christians in some science departments, such as the Earth Sciences Department in Cambridge, or the Physics Department in Oxford, is (apparently) higher than in the general population. But these scientist Christians generally hold not to postmodern forms of faith but rather to more traditional forms in which the evidential basis and historicity of their faith is emphasized. They really do believe that their religion is telling some deep truths about the world and about the human condition. Their suspicion of postmodernity is characteristic of both their science and their faith, and indeed I wonder whether this might help to explain why the level of Christian belief seems so much higher in the sciences than in the humanities.

Despite occasionally being a challenge to the science–religion dialogue, there are two ways in which I think postmodernism has had a positive influence. The first is due to the impact of postmodernism in the history and philosophy of science. It used to be the case that the religious beliefs and motivations of the natural philosophers who contributed to the emergence of modern science were simply ignored by historians, or else mentioned in passing as something rather incidental to their science. All that has now changed, helped along by the postmodern emphasis on the importance of individual thought within its particular cultural context, and the past few decades have seen some wonderful restorations of earlier natural philosophers to their full religious and cultural context.

Isaac Newton, for example, from my own university, was a passionate theist who saw his science as just one aspect of a great theological enterprise that also included ideas drawn from alchemy. Newton wrote far more about theology than he ever did about science, in fact around four million words on the subject that were never published during his life. Only now is the full collection of Newton's works being published online as part of the Newton Project based at the University of Sussex in the United Kingdom.[3] Many books have been published on Newton showing how, in his own mind, his theology and his alchemy were integral parts of his scientific endeavors.

The Darwin Festival took place in July 2009 in Cambridge to celebrate Darwin's bicentenary, with many of the world's leading evolutionary biologists speaking. It is interesting to note the openness of this Festival to theological discussion: for example, John Hedley Brooke and Daniel Dennett debated during one of the main plenary sessions, and there were two afternoon sessions on Darwinism and theology organized by the Cambridge Faculty of Divinity, when I spoke. I doubt there was such openness to theological debate and discussion within a scientific context at the last major Darwin centenary celebrations held in Chicago in 1959.

It is also interesting to note that academic positions in science and religion have developed in secular Western countries over the past decade or so in such universities as Oxford, Cambridge, Edinburgh, and Durham in Britain. The Faraday Institute for Science and Religion is part of my own College, St. Edmund's College, which in turn is part of Cambridge University. The study of the interactions between science and religion is now a respectable, if not all that common, aspect of academic life in Britain. I do not want to suggest that all these developments have occurred because of the impact of postmodernism on Western culture over the past few decades, but I do think postmodernism has helped to create a cultural climate in which such developments are now more acceptable within the secular academic environment.

A second positive impact of postmodernism is its critique of scientism. Scientism is the philosophy that suggests that the only reliable, objective form of knowledge is scientific knowledge. It is a derivative of positivism, long since dead and buried in philosophy departments, but scientism still lives on within some parts of the scientific community and in popular culture. So in this view science provides the facts, the reality, whereas religion is a matter of feelings and personal opinions.

One of the contributions of postmodernism is that it has provided ideas and a language that have helped to undermine this rather naïve view. The idea of different narratives is a familiar one within postmodern discourse, and this lends itself to some useful ways of relating scientific, religious, and other forms of knowledge.

We can imagine, for example, that the book of this complex entity called life (by which I mean the sum of all that we experience) is like a cube sliced into many layers. You need all the various levels of explanation to do justice to such a complex reality. In reality it is one book, but our brains are simply not up to the herculean task of grasping the book in its entirety all at one go.

So we have many different narratives: the scientific narrative tells us how things work and where they come from; the moral and ethical level addresses what we ought to do in the world; the aesthetic level gives insight into our understanding and appreciation of beauty; and so forth. One could add many more layers, not least the narrative provided by our own personal relationships. The religious narrative is addressing a different set of questions: Why is there a universe anyway? Does life have a purpose? Is there a God? And so on. Notice that these various narratives are in no sense rivals to each other; we need them all to do justice to our own experience as human agents. Such a model does not at all deny the complex interactions between each level, which are in no way isolated from each other, but only illustrates the obvious point that no one explanatory level or narrative is sufficient by itself. Scientism is just wrong: no one actually lives as if science provides the only valid form of well-justified knowledge and as if science is all we need.

The second main challenge to the science–religion dialogue comes from the rise of what is sometimes called the New Atheism. This is often associated with the biologist Richard Dawkins in the United Kingdom, and in the United States with people such as the philosopher Daniel Dennett, the writer Sam Harris, and the late journalist Christopher Hitchens, who have all recently written best-selling books that vigorously criticize religion. As it happens, their arguments are really very old—there is nothing new about their atheism. We also notice that the main proponents of the New Atheism are, with the exception of Sam Harris, quite old and that the new atheists are generally not practicing scientists—Dawkins left active science decades ago to become a scientific popularizer.

There are also many atheists who are not at all happy with books such as *The God Delusion* by Dawkins because they feel that he is letting the side down by publishing such poor arguments in support of atheism. As the atheist Darwinian philosopher Michael Ruse has commented: "*The God Delusion* made me ashamed to be an atheist."[4]

So what are the cultural forces driving the new atheists? I often think that cultural movements are like hurricanes that gain their energy by moving over warm seawater. The hotter the seawater, the more vigorous the hurricane becomes. So what is in the hot seawater to make the books of the new atheists such a publishing success? I suggest the following three factors.

First, 9/11 was a wake-up call to the atheists to realize what was already obvious to sociologists such as Peter Berger much earlier: that in fact societies don't necessarily become less religious as they modernize, as people once thought, and that religion in all its various forms was actually playing a major role in world affairs, and not always a very positive role. Second, the Bush administration was quite a religious regime in some ways and occasionally interfered in scientific research; in particular, Bush blocked federal funding of research into stem cells that involved the use of very early embryos. This greatly irritated the US scientific community and provided some further fuel for the atheistic backlash. Third, the ongoing popularity of creationism and intelligent design in the United States, with their legal attempts to get creationism or intelligent design taught as an alternative to evolution in American schools, has also greatly annoyed the scientific community.

Much of the rhetoric and polarization that typifies the New Atheism resonates with the increased alignment of religious commitment with the US Republican Party in contrast with the relatively secular Democrats, a significant and novel development in American life that has contributed to the growth of the so-called culture wars over the past two decades.[5]

Now how has the New Atheism impacted relationships between science and religion? Much of the impact has been negative in the following four ways. First, the new atheists have made the discussion very polarized in the media and in the public domain more widely. Religion is the enemy that must be attacked by any means. Emotional assertions take the place of rational arguments. The new atheists are not really interested in dialogue and do not know enough theology to have a serious engagement with ideas different from their own. In that respect, they are very different from an earlier, more educated, generation of atheists. Those moderate atheists, such as Michael Ruse, who "fraternize with the enemy"—meaning that they engage in sensible, academic dialogue with those from religious communities—are excoriated by the new atheists as compromising the true path of atheism. The new atheists tend to be rather shrill, engaging in a pejorative style of character assassination in a manner that tends to alienate most academics, whatever their own personal beliefs might be.

Second, the new atheists defend scientism and seek to invest science in general and evolution in particular with the rhetoric of atheism. As Dawkins writes: "I pay religions the compliment of regarding them as scientific theories and . . . I see God as a competing explanation for facts about the universe and life."[6] Within this approach, science and God are seen as offering rival accounts of the reality around us. With such a view, conflict between science and religion is of course the inevitable outcome. As Terry Eagleton, until recently professor of English literature at Manchester University, writes in *Reason, Faith and Revolution*: "Life for Dawkins would seem to divide neatly down the middle between things you can prove beyond all doubt, and blind faith. He fails to see that all the most interesting stuff goes on in neither of those places."[7]

Third, the god that the new atheists don't believe in is not really recognizable as the God of the Abrahamic faiths but rather as a god-of-the-gaps who is used to plug the gaps in current scientific ignorance. Thus, Christopher Hitchens writes in *God Is Not Great* that "thanks to the telescope and the microscope, [religion] no longer offers an explanation of anything important."[8] But Christianity was never meant to be an explanation of anything in the kind of way that telescopes and microscopes explain things. Quoting Eagleton again: "It's rather like saying that thanks to the electric toaster we can forget about Chekhov."[9] In Christian theology God is the ground of all being, not some causal factor to introduce as an explanation for a part of the cosmos that we do not yet understand very well in scientific terms.

Fourth, a negative impact of the New Atheism has been to stimulate the rise of creationism. If you keep telling people in the churches or the mosques that "evolution equals atheism," then of course it will not be surprising if religious believers find creationist alternatives more attractive. The new atheists are continuing in the long tradition of abusing science for ideological purposes.[10]

So all of these four factors impact negatively on the science–religion dialogue. On the other hand, every cloud has a silver lining, and the impact of the New Atheism has also provided some great opportunities for the science–religion dialogue. Three in particular stand out. First, the level of interest in the science–religion debate in the media has been raised. Because the media think that conflict sells, the coverage of the debate is not always very helpful, but at least the interest is there. A second and related point is that the general level of interest among the public has greatly increased due to the publicity given to the new atheists. At The Faraday Institute we organize regular short courses on science and religion. Since we started in 2006 by putting on six courses a year, we wondered whether interest might decline with the passage of time, but this has not happened; in fact, the number of delegates registering for our courses is higher than ever. I should also say in passing that we have been very happy to welcome a good number of Muslim delegates to our courses, which are open to those of any faith or of none. As staff from The Faraday Institute go out giving lectures, we find a very high level of interest in this topic, and if you put "Dawkins" in the title of your talk, then the numbers who come usually double. Controversy may have a negative side, but at least it arouses interest. A third positive spin-off from the New Atheism is the way that it has helped to make public discussion of theology quite respectable. Dawkins's Chair at Oxford, which he vacated recently, is actually a chair for the public understanding of science, although Dawkins really made it into a chair for antitheology. But the consequence, which I am sure was unintended, was that Dawkins's rhetoric has made it much more acceptable for scientists to discuss theology. Overall, then, the New Atheism has had some positive results for the science–religion dialogue.

The third challenge to the science–religion dialogue today comes from fundamentalism. The word "fundamentalism" has quite a long cultural and religious history, and in many ways it is not a very useful term. It tends to be used in journals of science such as *Nature* to refer to anyone who is anti-Darwinian.

Here I use the word to refer to Christians who read biblical texts as if they were scientific texts, and therefore believe either that the Bible teaches science or that modern scientific discoveries are prefigured in the Bible. This of course is the position of the young-earth Creationists who believe that the world was made less than ten thousand years ago in a period of six literal days of twenty-four hours. Henry Morris, one of the founders of this movement in the United States, saw the Bible as containing "scores of modern scientific truths, and no scientific errors," claiming that "the Scriptures, in fact, do not need to be 'interpreted' at all, for God is well able to say exactly what he means."[11]

Two points should be emphasized about creationism. First, it is a fruit of modernism, the idea that science provides the ultimate criteria for what is true. Creationism in the West is a twentieth-century movement that started in the United States in the 1920s and did not really emerge in its young-earth form until the early 1960s; the movement has grown to the point that today about 44 percent of the US population and 10 percent of the UK population are creationists.[12] Ironically, the creationist view of religious knowledge is actually very similar to that of the new atheists who also think that religious knowledge is in some kind of rivalry with scientific knowledge. That is why the media have often referred to Dawkins as a fundamentalist atheist, because in many ways the New Atheism and creationism provide mirror-image fundamentalisms. Opposite poles are often more similar to each other than either side would like to admit.

Second, creationism involves an understanding of the Bible that is quite different from traditional Jewish and Christian methods of interpretation. We have many commentaries on the creation passages in the early chapters of Genesis dating from the first to fifth centuries, but all commentators interpret these chapters figuratively. For example, in his commentary titled *The Literal Meaning of Genesis*, the final version of which was published in 415, Augustine saw God's creative activity as having two different aspects: "Some works belonged to the invisible days in which he created all things simultaneously, and others belong to the days in which he daily fashions whatever evolves in the course of time from what I call the primordial wrappers."[13] The "invisible days" in Augustine's exposition were the days as described in Genesis 1, which he understood not chronologically but as a kind of inventory of all God's acts of creation that were performed simultaneously. Out of this single act of creation eventually came all the rest of the diversity of the created order. Of course when Augustine uses the word translated as "evolves," we should not interpret that in its modern sense, but he did appear to believe that all of the potentiality of the created order was encompassed within those original "primordial wrappers" created by God in one instantaneous act. The point is not that we necessarily agree with Augustine in his interpretation of the text, but rather that such a sophisticated, figurative understanding of the text is typical of early Jewish and Christian commentators. Wooden literalism came much later.

The impact overall of fundamentalism on the science–religion dialogue has been negative. Because Christian fundamentalists are so hostile to evolution, this has understandably stimulated a very robust reaction from the scientific community. Because of the negative publicity given to creationism in the scientific press, it is very easy for secular scientists to think that all Christians are creationists. However, in my experience the reality is that nearly all Christians active in the biological sciences see no problem in holding together the biblical theology of creation with a strong commitment to the theory of evolution. The earliest written response to Darwin's *Origin of Species* in 1859 was a highly positive one, and it was from an Anglican cleric, Charles Kingsley.[14]

British historian James Moore writes that "with but few exceptions the leading Christian thinkers in Great Britain and America came to terms quite readily with Darwinism and evolution."[15] Similarly, American sociologist George Marsden reports that "with the exception of Harvard's Louis Agassiz, virtually every American Protestant zoologist and botanist accepted some form of evolution by the early 1870s."[16]

The challenge for the science–religion dialogue today is therefore one of education, both in science and in how to interpret the Bible. This is why I have recently written a book for Christians titled *Creation or Evolution—Do We Have to Choose?*[17] The answer is obviously no, we don't have to choose, but the challenge is to convey this message effectively to the Christian community. In the United Kingdom we are helped by several different societies that bring together science and faith, such as Christians in Science as well as the Science and Religion Forum; there are also the International Society for Science and Religion and other societies, all helping to show Christians and others that there is a "third way": evolution may be seen as the way in which God fulfills his intentions and purposes through the creative process.

I close with the words of an evolutionary biologist, Francis Collins, who used to be an atheist but who became a Christian in later life, and whose book *The Language of God* continues to be a bestseller. Until last year, Collins was the director of the National Human Genome Institute in Washington and was responsible for completing the sequencing of the human genome in 2003. Speaking of his experience as a Christian and as a scientist heading up arguably the most important project in contemporary biology, Collins has remarked that

> the work of a scientist involved in this project, particularly a scientist who has the joy of also being a Christian, is a work of discovery which can also be a form of worship. As a scientist, one of the most exhilarating experiences is to learn something . . . that no human has understood before. To have a chance to see the glory of creation, the intricacy of it, the beauty of it, is really an experience not to be matched. Scientists who do not have a personal faith in God also undoubtedly experience the exhilaration of discovery. But to have that joy of discovery, mixed together with the joy of worship, is truly a powerful moment for a Christian who is also a scientist.[18]

Notes

1. Peter Berger, "A Bleak Outlook Is Seen for Religion," *New York Times*, April 25, 1968, 3.

2. Peter L. Berger, "The Desecularization of the World: A Global Overview," in *The Desecularization of the World: Resurgent Religion and World Politics*, ed. Peter L. Berger (Grand Rapids, MI: Eerdmans, 1999), 2.

3. www.newtonproject.sussex.ac.uk.

4. Michael Ruse, "Dawkins et al Bring Us into Disrepute," *The Guardian*, November 2, 2009. www.guardian.co.uk/commentisfree/belief/2009/nov/02/atheism-dawkins-ruse.

5. R. D. Putnam and D. E. Campbell, *American Grace* (New York: Simon & Schuster, 2010).

6. Richard Dawkins, *River Out of Eden* (New York: HarperCollins, 1995), 46–47.

7. Terry Eagleton, *Reason, Faith and Revolution* (New Haven: Yale University Press, 2010), 6–7.

8. Christopher Hitchens, *God Is Not Great: How Religion Poisons Everything* (London: Atlantic Books, 2008), 282.

9. Eagleton, *Reason, Faith and Revolution*, 7.

10. Denis R. Alexander and Ronald L. Numbers, *Biology and Ideology—From Descartes to Dawkins* (Chicago: Chicago University Press, 2010).

11. H. M. Morris, *A Biblical Basis for Modern Science* (Grand Rapids: Baker, 1984), 47.

12. Nick Spencer and Denis Alexander, *Rescuing Darwin—God and Evolution in Britain Today* (London: Theos, 2009).

13. St. Augustine, *The Literal Meaning of Genesis*, vol. 1, tr. J. H. Taylor (New York: Paulist Press, 1982), 6.6.9.

14. Charles Kingsley, Letter to Charles Darwin, November 18, 1859. Cambridge: Darwin Correspondence Project, www.darwinproject.ac.uk/entry-2534. Accessed January 14, 2011.

15. J. Moore, *The Post-Darwinian Controversies: A Study of the Protestant Struggle to Come to Terms with Darwin in Great Britain and America, 1870–1900* (Cambridge: Cambridge University Press, 1981), 79.

16. George M. Marsden, "Understanding Fundamentalist Views of Science," in *Science and Creationism*, ed. Ashley Montagu (Oxford: Oxford University Press, 1984), 101.

17. Denis Alexander, *Creation or Evolution—Do We Have to Choose?* (Oxford: Monarch, 2008).

18. Quoted in D. R. Alexander and R. S. White, *Beyond Belief* (Oxford: Monarch, 2004), 84.

PART II

Texts and Commentaries

Biblical Texts

Creation as a source of revelation

Psalm 19:1–4a

[1]The heavens are telling the glory of God;
and the firmament proclaims his handiwork.
[2]Day to day pours forth speech,
and night to night declares knowledge.
[3]There is no speech, nor are there words;
their voice is not heard;
[4]yet their voice goes out through all the earth,
and their words to the end of the world.

Wisdom 13:1–5

[1]For all people who were ignorant of God were foolish by nature;
and they were unable from the good things that are seen to know the one who
    exists,
nor did they recognize the artisan while paying heed to his works;
[2]but they supposed that either fire or wind or swift air,
or the circle of stars, or turbulent water,
or the luminaries of heaven were the gods that rule the world.
[3]If through delight in the beauty of these things people assumed them to be
    gods,
let them know how much better than these is their Lord,
for the author of beauty created them.
[4]And if people were amazed at their power and working,
let them perceive from them
how much more powerful is the one who formed them.

[5]For from the greatness and beauty of created things
comes a corresponding perception of their Creator.

Romans 1:18–23

[18]For the wrath of God is revealed from heaven against all ungodliness and
wickedness of those who by their wickedness suppress the truth. [19]For what can
be known about God is plain to them, because God has shown it to them. [20]Ever
since the creation of the world his eternal power and divine nature, invisible
though they are, have been understood and seen through the things he has made.
So they are without excuse; [21]for though they knew God, they did not honor
him as God or give thanks to him, but they became futile in their thinking, and
their senseless minds were darkened. [22]Claiming to be wise, they became fools;
[23]and they exchanged the glory of the immortal God for images resembling a
mortal human being or birds or four-footed animals or reptiles.

Acts 17:24–29

[24]The God who made the world and everything in it, he who is Lord of heaven
and earth, does not live in shrines made by human hands, [25]nor is he served
by human hands, as though he needed anything, since he himself gives to all
mortals life and breath and all things. [26]From one ancestor he made all nations
to inhabit the whole earth, and he allotted the times of their existence and the
boundaries of the places where they would live, [27]so that they would search
for God and perhaps grope for him and find him—though indeed he is not
far from each one of us. [28]For "In him we live and move and have our being";
as even some of your own poets have said, "For we too are his offspring."

[29]Since we are God's offspring, we ought not to think that the deity is
like gold, or silver, or stone, an image formed by the art and imagination of
mortals.

Creation is in Christ

Colossians 1:9–10, 15–23

[9]For this reason, since the day we heard it, we have not ceased praying for you
and asking that you may be filled with the knowledge of God's will in all

spiritual wisdom and understanding, [10]so that you may lead lives worthy of the Lord, fully pleasing to him, as you bear fruit in every good work and as you grow in the knowledge of God. . . .

[15]He [Christ] is the image of the invisible God, the firstborn of all creation; [16]for in him all things in heaven and on earth were created, things visible and invisible, whether thrones or dominions or rulers or powers—all things have been created through him and for him. [17]He himself is before all things, and in him all things hold together. [18]He is the head of the body, the church; he is the beginning, the firstborn from the dead, so that he might come to have first place in everything. [19]For in him all the fullness of God was pleased to dwell, [20]and through him God was pleased to reconcile to himself all things, whether on earth or in heaven, by making peace through the blood of his cross.

[21]And you who were once estranged and hostile in mind, doing evil deeds, [22]he has now reconciled in his fleshly body through death, so as to present you holy and blameless and irreproachable before him—[23]provided that you continue securely established and steadfast in the faith, without shifting from the hope promised by the gospel that you heard, which has been proclaimed to every creature under heaven. I, Paul, became a servant of this gospel.

Humans within the community of creatures

Genesis 1:28–31

[28]God blessed them, and God said to them, "Be fruitful and multiply, and fill the earth and subdue it; and have dominion over the fish of the sea and over the birds of the air and over every living thing that moves upon the earth." [29]God said, "See, I have given you every plant yielding seed that is upon the face of all the earth, and every tree with seed in its fruit; you shall have them for food. [30]And to every beast of the earth, and to every bird of the air, and to everything that creeps on the earth, everything that has the breath of life, I have given every green plant for food." And it was so. [31]God saw everything that he had made, and indeed, it was very good. And there was evening and there was morning, the sixth day.

1 Kings 4:29–34

²⁹God gave Solomon very great wisdom, discernment, and breadth of understanding as vast as the sand on the seashore, ³⁰so that Solomon's wisdom surpassed the wisdom of all the people of the east, and all the wisdom of Egypt. ³¹He was wiser than anyone else, wiser than Ethan the Ezrahite, and Heman, Calcol, and Darda, children of Mahol; his fame spread throughout all the surrounding nations. ³²He composed three thousand proverbs, and his songs numbered a thousand and five. ³³He would speak of trees, from the cedar that is in the Lebanon to the hyssop that grows in the wall; he would speak of animals, and birds, and reptiles, and fish. ³⁴People came from all the nations to hear the wisdom of Solomon; they came from all the kings of the earth who had heard of his wisdom.

Ecclesiastes 3:18–22

¹⁸I said in my heart with regard to human beings that God is testing them to show that they are but animals. ¹⁹For the fate of humans and the fate of animals is the same; as one dies, so dies the other. They all have the same breath, and humans have no advantage over the animals; for all is vanity. ²⁰All go to one place; all are from the dust, and all turn to dust again. ²¹Who knows whether the human spirit goes upward and the spirit of animals goes downward to the earth? ²²So I saw that there is nothing better than that all should enjoy their work, for that is their lot; who can bring them to see what will be after them?

Ecclesiastes 11:5–6

⁵Just as you do not know how the breath comes to the bones in the mother's womb, so you do not know the work of God, who makes everything. ⁶In the morning sow your seed, and at evening do not let your hands be idle; for you do not know which will prosper, this or that, or whether both alike will be good.

Commentary

ELLEN F. DAVIS

A PRIMARY QUESTION that informs all the texts is epistemological: How do we gain accurate knowledge of God and the world? Three initial observations highlight the connections among them:

1. Most of the texts, while focusing on what is viewed as the elect community, Israel, or the church, pose that question in the broader context of all humanity or even (in Colossians) the whole community of creatures vis-à-vis their Creator.

2. A further insight and question that might be explored through the collection of texts concerns how knowledge may be variously related to moral character. True knowledge is edifying: it builds up human character. Conversely, ignorance or false wisdom damages it, even fatally. Furthermore, the state of ignorance may itself be culpable, "without excuse," as two of our texts describe those who lack true knowledge of God.

3. The texts are divided into three topics: "creation as a source of revelation," "creation in Christ," and "humans within the community of creatures." Those three topics might be related as denoting the concentric contexts in which humans are embedded, as we seek (or purport) to know God. That is, humans are embedded within creation, and creation is in turn embedded in Christ; at the same time, creation is a community of witness to God through the gospel of Jesus Christ.

In what follows I treat the several texts by topic, beginning with "Creation as a source of revelation." It is notable that the four texts in this section may span a period of more than a millennium of ancient Near Eastern religious insight, if (as many suppose) Psalm 19 has its origins in a second millennium

53

Canaanite hymn to the sun god. If so, the hymn was subsequently adapted to the monotheistic claims of Israel's faith and amplified by a subsequent section (omitted here) devoted to revelation through Torah. The bright sun and the nighttime sky offered the ancients of the Levant unmistakable evidence of the existence of a glorious high god attended by *ṣĕbā'ôt*, heavenly armies ("hosts," in traditional English). Like Genesis 1, this hymn clearly designates the heavenly bodies as creatures rather than deities.[1] But if in Genesis they are little more than light fixtures (*mĕ'ōrōt*), here the heavens with their steady markers of day and night are articulate creatures that "discharge utterance" (v. 3), albeit wordless utterance. Thus they bear witness to God throughout the whole world. The second half of the psalm uses images of light to draw out the crucial implication of that for Israel: Torah with the commandments "enlightens the eyes" (v. 9); it is a source of light, like the heavenly bodies themselves.

The next two texts, Wisdom 13 and Romans 1, both come from Hellenized Jews writing after the Roman conquest of the East in 30 BCE: the anonymous author of Wisdom, from Alexandria in Egypt, and his younger (probably) contemporary, the Apostle Paul from Tarsus in Asia.[2] The author of Wisdom identifies as "mindless" (*mataioi*) those who fail to see that the beauty and power of material things are not direct markers of divinity but rather pointers to the invisible and even more glorious *Technitis*, the master Craftsman who produced these things. Those who have sufficient intellectual power to investigate material things should come to true religious insight; if they ultimately fail to do so, they are without excuse (vv. 7–9). Nonetheless, the tone of the whole passage is less condemnatory than inviting; the author judges with some sympathy those who err (temporarily) out of a genuine desire to find God (v. 6).

Paul denounces that same error more quickly and harshly: there is no excuse for "the ungodliness and wickedness of those who by their wickedness suppress the truth" (Rom 1:18). "Ever since the creation of the world" humans have had the opportunity to know God truly "through the things that he has made" (v. 20). One of the universal benefits of reason is the potential to move from observation of the creatures to perception of the Creator. Perhaps Paul's greatest insight here is to link knowledge with gratitude. True knowledge is activated only through honoring and giving thanks to God; humble gratitude keeps the knower in a life of righteousness (cf. 1:17). By contrast, false knowledge ultimately darkens the mind by pride and thus becomes a source of foolishness.

The final text in this section, from the book of Acts, strikes a different note. This is the second book written by Luke the Evangelist; it recounts the work of Jesus' disciples and apostles, and especially Paul, following the death and resurrection of their Lord. In chapter 17, Paul is in Athens, the epicenter of the Greek thought world. He argued in synagogues and marketplaces, where Epicurean and Stoic philosophers debated with him. Here we see him speaking to those gathered at the Areopagus ("field of Mars," where the city council met) to hear whatever teaching was new and "hot" (v. 21). Although Luke tells us that Paul "was deeply distressed to see that the city was full of idols" (v. 16), he does not denounce the Greeks for their wickedness (as we might have expected from Romans 1). Instead Paul appeals to insight found already within their tradition of philosophical poetry, citing the assertion (possibly of Epimenides, from the sixth century) that "in [God] we live and move and have our being"—a somewhat ambiguous variant of the common Stoic teaching that a divine Logos (reason or mind) animates the world as a living creature.[3] Paul also cites the image from the third-century poet Aratus (who came from Paul's own region, Cilicia), that we humans are God's "offspring." His hearers (and Luke's readers) would have recognized that both Greek statements are broadly compatible with the biblical creation story, which represents humans as made in God's image and receiving breath directly from God, and also with the biblical writers' frequent use of the metaphor of divine parenthood: God is like a father, or sometimes a mother, to Israel. Paul's point would seem to be that a good philosophical anthropology is the basis for good theology. At least it eliminates certain absurdities, such as the notion that "the deity is like gold, or silver, or stone, an image formed by the art and imagination of mortals" (v. 29).

The text under the heading "Creation is in Christ" clarifies the relation between the various creatures and God, and the nature of God's true image. Although written in Paul's name, the Letter to the Colossians is often thought to come from a disciple who, after the Apostle's death, continued his ministry of teaching in Asia Minor. Regardless of whether its author knew Acts (which is doubtful), the hymn in the first chapter stands within the New Testament as a complement to Paul's teaching in Athens, showing how it is that all creatures "live and move and have [their] being" in God—namely, through Christ, metaphorically called "the firstborn of all creation." Several other points might be highlighted:

1. Fruitful knowledge of God is given by the grace of God as a response to prayer.

2. Christ is the true image of God, and all the creatures "in heaven and on earth" were created in and for Christ, in whom "all things hold together" (v. 17). That is a statement about what we might now call the original biotic pyramid, and further about the reconciliation of all creatures to their Creator. The notion that the whole created order "whether on earth or in heaven" needs to be reconciled with God stands against such stories as the cursing of the soil following the first disobedience in Eden; the extension of violence and corruption through the whole earth, which culminates in the flood but is not ended by it (Gen 6:11–13 and 9:21); and the rebellion among the angelic beings to which Jesus refers in Luke's Gospel: "I watched Satan fall from heaven like a flash of lightning" (10:18).

3. Following from the understanding that all creation is in Christ, the passage makes the most inclusive evangelistic statement in the Bible: the gospel of Christ was in fact "proclaimed to every creature under heaven" (v. 23). The claim that the gospel is for the nonhuman creatures no less than for humans is radically challenging of a modern rationalistic sensibility, but it accords with Psalm 19 and other poetic images of the nonhuman creatures responding to God's voice (Ps 29) and offering witness and praise (Ps 96, 98, 148).

The "ecological" understanding of the unity of creation in Christ in this passage from Colossians is amplified in various ways by the texts in the final section, "Humans within the community of creatures." The first and last verses selected from Genesis 1 are among the most familiar in the entire Bible. The first establishes that humans are to exercise "skilled mastery among" the creatures (a translation that does equal justice to the Hebrew as the conventional "have dominion over," and may be less misleading in contemporary context). The last states that God judges the whole creation to be "very good." It is curious, then, that the intervening two verses (29 and 30) are virtually overlooked by modern commentators with respect to their possible theological significance. Biblical writers often use simple juxtaposition to establish a connection, and so we may suppose that these verses supply content for what precedes, namely the otherwise unspecified charge for humans to exercise skilled mastery among the creatures. Immediately following that charge, God points to the abundance of the food supply, sufficient for every creature. It would seem that skilled mastery has something to do with sustaining all that material goodness, the abundance of which is such a pronounced emphasis of this chapter. An abundance of plants that are nutritious for humans is one of the distinctive biological features of the uplands of Western Asia, and this was an enabling condition for the agricultural experiments that began there twelve thousand years ago. In short scientific terms, it seems that we are to maintain the health of the food chains, that is, to maintain biodiversity. Living as we do now in the Sixth Great Age of Extinction on our planet, of which humans themselves are the chief driving force, these verses would seem to speak a strong word of judgment about our fulfillment of the original divine charge.

The passage from Kings (dating from approximately the seventh century BCE, in Judah) outlines briefly the scope of the "wisdom," the intellectual and cultural tradition that contributed importantly to the prestige of royal courts in the ancient Near East. Solomon's wisdom includes both the social realm (the normal province of proverbial wisdom) and the natural phenomena. While we are told that his wisdom is God-given, that does not exclude the operation of empirical observation. He is meant to exercise "discernment (*těbûnâ*), and breadth of understanding (literally, 'heart')" (1 Kgs 5:9; Heb 4:29 Eng.), based on patient and accurate observation of both social dynamics and natural phenomena.

The author of Ecclesiastes is known as Qohelet, who was evidently a teacher of relatively privileged boys or young men in Hellenistic Jerusalem. Writing about the middle of the third century BCE, Qohelet is the earliest known Jewish writer to position himself consciously vis-à-vis both Greek philosophy (including natural philosophy) and biblical tradition. He is the great debunker within the biblical tradition, skeptical of all human pretensions. In Ecclesiastes 3, he develops the "dust to dust" image from Genesis (3:19) in a way that minimizes human uniqueness as represented in Genesis 1. The second passage, from Ecclesiastes 11, points to one of the fundaments of Qohelet's understanding of wisdom—namely, recognition of the limits of human knowledge, both religious and natural. God is for him, as for the poets of Genesis and the Psalms, the one "who makes everything" (11:5). However, in contrast to Paul (in Romans 1) and the author of the Wisdom of Solomon, Qohelet asserts that relatively little of God's work is transparent to us. His characteristic response to the limits of human knowledge is evident in both passages: do your humble daily work properly. The work he specifies is that of the average Israelite, sowing seed. Qohelet's thought often returns to Genesis; it is intriguing, therefore, that in advising his students about how to make the best use of their limited knowledge, he points to the same essential work implied by Genesis 1: maintaining by our skilled efforts the fruitfulness of God's originally abundant creation.

For Further Reflection

1. What attitudes to the possibility and desirability of studying the created order do these texts encourage?
2. In what light do these texts depict the relationship between humans and other creatures, and how does this bear on Christian approaches to understanding and relating to the created order?
3. How (if at all) does belief in Christ as the one in whom "all things hold together" shape Christian approaches to understanding and exploring the created order?
4. What other biblical texts could have been selected for discussion here, perhaps because they have historically been significant in shaping Christian attitudes to scientific work?

Notes

1. See the essay by Michael Welker in this volume.

2. David Winston dates the Wisdom of Solomon to the reign of Caligula (37–41 CE); see David Winston, *The Wisdom of Solomon* (Anchor Bible; New York: Doubleday, 1979), 3. James Reese proposes a date near the beginning of the reign of Augustus Caesar's reign in 28 BCE; see James Reese, "Wisdom of Solomon," *Harper's Bible Commentary*, ed. James L. Mays (San Francisco: Harper & Row, 1988), 821.

3. Carl Holladay states that the saying "reverses the usual pantheistic Stoic assertion of divine immanence." Carl Holladay, "Acts," *Harper's Bible Commentary*, ed. James L. Mays (San Francisco: Harper & Row, 1988), 1103.

What Is Creation?

Subtle Insights from Genesis 1
Concerning the Order of the World

MICHAEL WELKER

To BEGIN, LET US LOOK AT how today's general dictionaries understand the word "creation." They define creation as "nature," the "world," or a vaguely conceived "totality," provided that it is understood as dependent or having been brought about by higher powers. These motifs of being "brought about" or "dependent" persist regardless whether that creation (*creatura*) is attributed to one god or multiple gods, or even other more primary, manifestly superior or otherworldly, supernatural powers or authorities. However, even the activity of bringing about such a "whole," the world or nature is described as "creation" (*creatio*). And yet the concluding ideas and concepts about this act of "bringing about," and that which has been generated, remain mostly opaque. These "final thoughts" circulate in myths and sagas, and in almost indecipherable cosmological theories.[1]

For some time now in our Western cultures, these ideas have been drawn together and reduced to a very abstract and meager conception, that of a primal cause or of "being caused," a conception behind which one can neither venture nor inquire: God is "the ground of all being," "the all-determining reality," "the ultimate point of reference," and so on. These overly simplistic theistic ideas lead many among us to equally simplistic questions and concerns such as, "How can such an omnipotent and good God allow suffering?" In contrast to this, however, we find a much more subtle picture painted by the so-called Priestly Creation narrative in Genesis 1, the most important classical text among the Bible's Creation stories.

Probably composed during the Babylonian exile around the year 550 BCE (586–538), this text picks up and processes significantly older Creation myths

59

from the Ancient Near East. It is a classic on the topic of "Creation"—a topic that we also find treated in Genesis 2, various Psalms, and in texts of the wisdom traditions. When we thematize the apparent inconsistencies of Genesis 1, it becomes strikingly clear that this biblical Creation narrative actually contains a very nuanced understanding of reality, which should be illuminating and challenging not only for the theological but also for the scientific mind.

Let us start with the first of these seeming inconsistencies, which can appear in the tension between Genesis 1:3–5 and Genesis 1:14ff. On the one hand, we read in verses 3–5 that "God said, 'Let there be light,' and there was light. God saw that the light was good, and he separated the light from the darkness. And God called the light 'day,' and the darkness he called 'night.' And there was evening, and there was morning—the first day."[2] On the other hand, we discover verses 14–19 thematizing the creation of heavenly bodies that are themselves tasked with separating day and night. How can God create light without involving the sun and stars? Why does the separation of day and night occur twice? Is this achieved directly by God, or are the heavenly bodies supposed to divide day and night? While such questions seem to offer clever objections to the supposed naiveté of a text unable to express its own ideas, they actually fail to perceive the subtle understanding of reality being developed here.

The Priestly Creation narrative operates with two temporal systems, the first being the days of God, and the second being the days of this world that are set in rhythm by heavenly bodies. Referring to the work of the great Jewish scholar Benno Jacob, the influential Heidelberg Old Testament scholar Claus Westermann, and other colleagues, the Zurich Old Testament scholar Odil Hannes Steck has shown that two perspectives on reality and two time systems must be distinguished here.[3] God thus creates brightness, transparency, and light from the very beginning. In the divine activity of creating, God acts in this brightness.[4] The light of God, the light in which God creates, rests, and is alive and effective, is not simply identical with the light in which human beings and other creatures live. They stand, though, in analogy to each other. This analogical relation is what makes it possible at all for there to be knowledge of God and of creation under the conditions of earthly existence. Likewise, the separation of light from darkness, carried out by God in the first work of Creation, is far from simply identical with the separation of day from night by means of the stars. Yet there are analogies between God's days and the days of creatures.

Of course, the composers of the Priestly Creation narrative did not have access to our modern cosmological knowledge. The largest possible number conceivable by the authors of the Old Testament was probably that which appears in Daniel 7:10, which, describing the heavenly host before God, speaks of "ten thousand times ten thousand [standing] before him." Thirteen billion years was not even conceivable for the biblical authors—we ourselves have only been operating with this concept since the twentieth century. Yet while the biblical texts draw an analogy between God's time and "time under heaven," they also distinguish between them, as is clear from statements such as in Psalm 90:4: "For a thousand years in your sight are like a day that has just gone by, or like a watch in the night."

God's days are great temporal units within which we find the creation of a finely differentiated correlation between that range of various realities and life processes that we today divide into cosmological, biological, cultural, and religious processes. The activity of creation demonstrates itself in the complex connection of these very different fields of life and action. In the act of creation we see the establishment of complex interdependencies between various spheres of life. Indeed, strictly speaking, it is only in their designation for one another and in the process of their mutual interweaving that these cosmic, biological, cultural, and religious spheres of life become "creation."

The subtlety of the Priestly Creation narrative is revealed again via a second seeming inconsistency. On the one hand, we read that God separates, brings forth, creates, places, and so on. On the other hand, the text often uses the same verbs (separating, ruling, bringing forth, developing, reproducing) to assign this activity to creatures. This differentiated self-activity by created beings is repeatedly placed in parallel with God's own creative work, yet without it ceasing to be the self-activity of creatures. Thus the firmament of heaven is charged with separating the waters and creating and maintaining space for the further formation and development of creatures (Gen 1:6). But in the following verse we read that it is God who made the firmament and separated the waters. (Gen 1:7). The lights of that firmament are to rule over day and night and separate light from darkness (Gen 1:14). Yet in parallel, we read that God made the lights, and God sets those lights in the firmament (Gen 1:16–18). Verses 21 and 25 stress that God creates all kinds of land animals, but here too we find an appeal to the generative power of the earth: "And God said, 'Let the land produce living creatures according to their kinds: livestock, creatures that move along the ground, and wild animals'" (Gen 1:24). Thus, according to the Priestly Creation narrative, creation and evolution are not alternatives. For many scientists and people influenced by belief in merely scientific worldviews, evolution is regarded as "the most efficient engine of atheism ever discovered by humans." "Creationists and believers in almost any religion are right that evolutionary biology should be feared and rejected. It is the great engine of atheism."[5]

Yet, as a third seeming inconsistency prompts us to ask, how are we to distinguish between God and creature, God's creativity and power, and the creaturely creativities and powers? This question becomes quite urgent when we begin to think of God and world, God and creature, in a one-to-one relationship—as is, unfortunately, all too characteristic for most popular and even some educated religious thinking. How can we distinguish God and world, God and the human being, when God, world, and person are all co-creative entities? The answer is that a mere one-to-one relationship is precisely what we do not find represented in biblical Creation-thought. Rather, we have to reflect a one-to-many relationship. Different creatures share in God's creativity, but in a graduated way. The heavens separate, the stars rule, the earth brings forth, and human beings receive the so-called call to dominion. Yet God is the one who orchestrates these various dimensions and processes. As soon as we understand this model it becomes clear why biblical thought relates God's creation with God's rule. The cooperation between different spheres of life and created realms of power is attributed and credited to divine activity.

A deeper recognition of the concept of world order in the Priestly text arises from a fourth seeming inconsistency that is summed up in the following question: If creatures are given a share in God's creativity, does this not then endanger creation; that is, does creation not then potentially endanger itself? Furthermore, if the self-endangerment of creation is actually permitted, how can the Bible say that creation is "good"; indeed, how can we say together with verse 31: "God saw all that he had made, and it was very good. And there was evening, and there was morning—the sixth day"?

This common question is often connected with the issue of theodicy: How can we reconcile suffering and death in creation with the goodness and power of God? There is a very clear, yet equally sobering, answer to this question:

creation does not offer us a life of divine glory. Creatures are not divine beings. In contrast to other Creation narratives from the Ancient Near East, the biblical Creation story actually brings about a secularization of the powers of heaven, the stars, the earth, and even the monsters of the deep. Even the heavens are no longer a divine entity but rather a creature. From the perspective of the biblical traditions, they are a powerful creature since the forces of light, warmth, and water come to earth "from the heavens." But they are not to be worshipped. In the same way, the stars are powerful not only as natural beings but also as culturally determinative forces. They regulate time and the dates of festivals.

But even the stars are not to be worshipped as gods, as was common in other ancient religions. And while other Creation narratives from the Ancient Near East speak of a battle between God, or the gods, and the forces of chaos (arising, for example, from the depths of the sea), in verses 20–21 we read God's command: "Let the water teem with living creatures, and let birds fly above the earth above the expanse of the sky. So God created the great creatures of the sea and every living and moving thing with which the water teems." Talk of great sea creatures (which Luther translated as "whales") hints at those monsters of the deep seen in other Creation narratives, monsters against which the gods must battle in order to create. But in the biblical Creation account, the great monsters are naturalized and secularized. All these most impressive and sometimes frightening creatures are not gods, even though they possess great power. Yet with that power they can also cause conflicts and risks in creation.

We see this especially clearly in the charge of dominion given to human beings: "God blessed them and said to them, 'Be fruitful and increase in number; fill the earth and subdue it. Rule over the fish of the sea and the birds of the air and over every living creature that moves on the ground'" (Gen 1:28). The verbs "to subdue" and "to rule" speak the language of conquerors and of slaveholders. In the 1960s and 1970s, this led to a naïve conception that the biblical Creation narratives sponsored ecological brutalism, particularly evident in Descartes naming the human being "maître et possesseur de la nature." In response to this accusation, some offered an equally naïve theology that sought to concentrate more upon the so-called Yahwist Creation narrative in Genesis 2, thus emphasizing that narrative's language of "cultivating and keeping" the earth as an apparently more appropriate approach to Creation—as if the good gardener would not go into the garden or field with secateurs and hoe.

Over against such maneuvering, we can clearly see that the Priestly Creation narrative in Genesis 1 expressly addresses this problem: that human beings as well as animals are both allocated to a communal sphere for nutrition, and thus it will come to a conflict of interests. In the call to dominion, this conflict is clearly decided in favor of human beings. We have here a distinct anthropocentrism in defiance of all nature worship. Yet neither do we have unchecked brutalism against our fellow creatures. Again, this is made clear in the famous text on the calling of human beings to reflect the *imago Dei*, the image of God: "So God created man in his own image, in the image of God he created him; male and female he created them" (Gen 1:27). This language of the *imago Dei* stems from royal ideology of the Ancient Near East and is connected with the expectation that a ruler will practice justice and defend the weak. Thus the Priestly Creation narrative develops a subtle ethos regarding the status of human dominion. On the one hand, there is an endorsement of human reproduction and expansion across the earth, and humans are privileged over the animals. On the other hand, humans are to reflect the *imago Dei*; that is, they should rule as the image of God, guaranteeing justice and providing protection for the weak—not only among human beings but also for the rest of creation.

These tensions help us to recognize the way in which the Creation narrative is very realistically aware of a world in which life lives off other life. It is not a dream world or utopia but the world in which we actually find ourselves. Yet the next seeming inconsistency prompts us to object: How can it then be that "God saw that it was good"—indeed, even "very good"? In the Old Testament, "good" (*ṭôb*) means that which "supports and promotes life." Thus, the orchestrated interplay of cosmic, biological, cultural, and religious processes is seen by God as good, as that which truly nurtures life. Yet, again, this does not mean that creation offers us a life of divine glory. There remains a sharp distinction between God and creation. The conflicts that subsequently arise from this situation, especially in the struggle between human beings and animals, are taken up in the Priestly Creation narrative and regulated by the charge to dominion and through the special distinction of human beings as the *imago Dei*.

Sadly, human beings are in no position to live up to that distinction. The book of Genesis already highlights the potential for massive self-endangerment, delusion, and self-destruction—themes that are extensively developed in the stories of the so-called primal history that follow the Creation narrative. "Creation" alone cannot testify adequately to the divinity of God. A merely naturalistic perception of creation is totally insufficient. Yet even an "expansion" of this focus on nature to include aspects of "culture and history" will remain theologically deficient as long as it fails to offer perspectives on the salvific and redemptive work of God.[6]

Notes

1. See Michael Welker, *Creation and Reality: Theological and Biblical Perspectives, Warfield Lectures 1991* (Philadelphia: Fortress Press, 1999).

2. Biblical passages are from the New Revised Standard Version, with some adaptations by the author.

3. Odil Hannes Steck, *Der Schöpfungsbericht der Priesterschrift: Studien zur literarkritischen und überlieferungsgeschichtlichen Problematik von Genesis 1,1–2,4a*, rev. ed. (Göttingen: Vandenhoeck & Ruprecht, 1981), 112–13 and 161ff.

4. See ibid., 176.

5. William B. Provine, "Evolution, Religion, and Science," in *The Oxford Handbook of Religion and Science*, ed. Philip Clayton (Oxford: Oxford University Press, 2006), 667–80, at 667 and 679; a more nuanced perspective with respect to the enormous suffering in the universe is given by John F. Haught, "God and Evolution," in ibid., 697–712.

6. See Michael Welker, *The Science and Theology Dialogue: What Can Theology Contribute?* (Neukirchen: Neukirchener Verlag, 2012).

Qur'ānic Texts

HE IS THE ORIGINATOR of the heavens and the earth, and when He decrees something, He says only "Be," and it is. (2:117)

Your Lord is God, who created the heavens and earth in six Days, then established Himself on the throne—He makes the night cover the day in swift pursuit; He created the sun, moon and stars to be subservient to His command; all creation and command belong to Him—exalted be God, Lord of all the worlds! (7:54)

It is God who created seven heavens, and a similar [number] of earths. His commandment descends throughout them. So you should realize that He has power over all things and that His knowledge encompasses everything. (65:12)

Everything that is in the heavens and earth glorifies God; all control and praise belong to Him; He has power over everything. (64:1)

In the creation of the heavens and the earth; in the alternation of night and day; in the ships that sail to the sea with goods for people; in the water which God sends down from the sky to give life to the earth where it has been barren, scattering all kinds of creatures over it; in the changing of the winds and clouds that run their appointed courses between the sky and earth: there are signs in all these for those who use their minds. (2:164)

There is a sign for them in the lifeless earth. We give it life and We produce grain from it for them to eat. We have put gardens of date palms and grapes in the earth, and We have made springs of water gush out of it so that they could eat its fruit. It was not their own hands that made all this. How can they not give thanks? (36:33–35)

We shall show them Our signs in every region of the earth and in themselves, until it becomes clear to them that this is the Truth. Is it not enough that your Lord witnesses everything? (41:53)

Who is it who made the earth a stable place to live? Who made rivers flow through it? Who set immovable mountains on it and created a barrier between the fresh and salt water? Is it another god beside God? No! But most of them do not know. (27:61)

Do they not see the sky above them—how We have built and adorned it, with no rifts in it? (50:6)

It is God who raised up the heavens with no visible supports and then established Himself on the throne; He has subjected the sun and the moon each to pursue its course for an appointed time; He regulates all things and makes the revelations clear so that you may be certain of meeting your Lord; it is He who spread out the earth, placed firm mountains and rivers on it, and made two of every kind of fruit; He draws the veil of night over the day. There truly are signs in this for people who reflect. (13:2–3)

It is He who made the sun a shining radiance and the moon a light, determining phases for it so that you might know the number of years and how to calculate time—God did not create all these without a true purpose; He explains his signs to those who understand. (10:5)

God keeps the heavens and earth from vanishing; if they did vanish, no one else could stop them. God is most forbearing, most forgiving. (35:41)

If there had been in the heavens or earth any gods but Him, both heavens and earth would be in ruins: God, Lord of the Throne, is far above the things they say. (21:22)

It was He who created all that is on the earth for you; He turned to the sky and made the seven heavens; it is He who has knowledge of all things. (2:29)

Do the disbelievers not see how rain clouds are formed, how the heavens are lifted, how the mountains are raised high; how the earth is spread out? (88:17–20)

There truly are signs in the creation of the heavens and earth, and in the alternation of night and day, for those with understanding, who remember God standing, sitting and lying down, who reflect on the creation of the heavens and earth: "Our Lord! You have not created all this without purpose—You are far above that!—so protect us from the torment of the Fire." (3:190–91)

Jinn and mankind, if you can pass beyond the regions of heaven and earth, then do so: you will not pass without Our authority. Which, then, of your Lord's blessings do you both deny? (55:33–34)

Say: "See what is in the heavens and on the earth." But what use are signs and warnings to people who will not believe? (10:101)

Are the disbelievers not aware that the heavens and the earth used to be joined together and that We ripped them apart, that We made every living thing from water—will they not believe?—and we put firm mountains on the earth, lest it should sway under them, and set broad paths on it, so they might follow the right direction, and We made the sky a well-secured canopy—yet from its wonders they turn away. (21:30–33)

M. A. S. Abdel Haleem, *The Qur'an: A New Translation* (Oxford University Press, 2004).

Commentary

MUSTANSIR MIR

THE ABSENCE OF A HISTORICAL CONFLICT between science and Islam has led some, perhaps many, Muslims to believe that, unlike Christianity, Islam faces no challenge from science today. But the largely secularist orientation, premises, and parameters of the modern scientific enterprise are fundamentally different from the orientation, premises, and parameters of science in ancient, medieval, and premodern times. Of course, an easy way of heading off a possible conflict between science and religion is to raise the entirely valid question of the limits of scientific discourse and argue that religion and science each have a different province of activity and each speak a different language. From a practical standpoint, however, it cannot be denied that scientists, too, have their views and opinions, and that what they think—or even speculate—contributes, for good or ill, to the creation of an intellectual climate. And it is difficult to deny that, in the particular context in which science is prosecuted today, the net effect of the scientists' excogitations is to create the impression that science and religion are in conflict, with science being the privileged route to the ascertainment of truth in the philosophical sphere no less than in the scientific sphere proper. It is in this sense that any challenge that science poses to religion is posed to all—or at least to the so-called theistic—religions.

When, with this background in mind, we look at the Qur'ānic texts presented in this volume, we wonder how these texts can at all be relevant to an investigation of the science–religion dialectic at which the whole volume aims. We are faced with the question: Are we trying to draw from the Qur'ān answers it was never meant to provide? How can a series of statements or claims, made in an imperious tone, illuminate a subject that calls for rational inquiry? It is important to bear in mind that this selection of texts does not constitute the entirety of the Qur'ān. Viewed as a whole, the Qur'ān not only states and prescribes but also seeks to validate, with reasons and arguments, a set of ideas and concepts that have internal coherence and contribute to the creation of a distinctive worldview and a specific code of guidance. Setting our texts within the larger context of the Qur'ānic universe of ideas is, then, part of our challenge. Instead of commenting in detail on any particular texts, we will offer some general observations.

The God Question

The first thing that jumps out at the reader of these texts is the centrality of God in them. The texts speak of a personal God who is the originator of the heavens and the earth, who, as supreme sovereign, controls and manages all of creation. In other words, there is simply no way of ducking the God question. The centrality of God—of a personal God—in the Qur'ān has to be reckoned with in any discussion of religion and science from an Islamic viewpoint. As in Judaism and Christianity, the existence of God—of a being who, ultimately, is in charge of the world—is assumed in Islam. But in the Qur'ān, the real purpose of the emphasis placed on God's sovereignty and control over nature (perhaps a better word than "world" or "universe" in the present context) is to underscore the idea that nature's involuntary submission to God constitutes an object lesson for human beings, who ought to make voluntary submission to God if they wish to achieve in their lives the peace and harmony found in nature on account of nature's submission to God. The point to note in the Qur'ānic texts, though, is that human submission is predicated on study of and reflection on the many and multifarious phenomena—or "signs"—that make up nature.

Nature as a Repository of Signs

Nature, then, is a repository of signs. The word "sign" (*āya*) is a key word in the texts. Two things need to be noted about a sign. First, by definition, a sign points to something beyond itself, the signifier being a means used to arrive at the signified, the latter occupying a higher ontological status. It would be a mistake to focus attention on the signifier at the cost of neglecting the signified. Equally, however, it would be a mistake to bypass the signifier in an attempt to reach the signified. Study of nature as a repository of signs is mandated, therefore, in the Qur'ān. Second, a sign is marked by a certain ambiguity; a sign, these texts repeatedly say, will yield its meaning only to "people who reflect," "those who use their minds," and this meaning will be lost on those who fail to reflect or use their minds. Discovery of the meaning of a sign is neither inevitable nor automatic.

Two Approaches to Nature

Nature is the province of scientific investigation, and nature is the main subject in these Qur'ānic texts. The difference between the scientific and scriptural approaches to nature is starkly apparent: while science seeks to study and explain the structure of nature, scripture seeks to discover the significance of nature; to use an analogy, science focuses on the body of nature, whereas scripture focuses on the spirit of nature. Both science and religion are preoccupied with the regularity, order, and stability of nature, but these phenomena lead science to derive one set of conclusions, and lead religion to derive what religion would call a higher order of conclusions, since these conclusions are supposed to be built on the order of conclusions that may be called scientific. In other words, the mandate of religion goes beyond the mandate of science.

Human Response

The Qur'ānic texts in question are not meant to be a cold description or a dispassionate analysis of nature; they aim to elicit an active response from human beings, their addressees. The desired response, presented in these texts as logical and warranted, consists in recognizing God as the central, ultimate reality and submitting to His command, for, as one of the verses says, "all creation and command belong to Him" (7:54). The need for human beings to submit to God has been underlined earlier. Two more points may be noted here. First, the texts under study address all of humanity, not a particular segment of humanity with special credentials or qualifications. Second, they invite the addressees not to visit a scientific laboratory but to participate in a reality that surrounds them immediately: the tools of religious reflection are not necessarily the telescope and the microscope but rather a responsive mind and a feeling heart. The texts are motivational in the sense that they aim to actuate the human mind and stir the human heart so as to enable human beings to make the desired response to the beckoning signs of nature.

For Further Reflection

1. How does the notion of a personal God square with the scientific worldview? Central to the discussion of this issue is the question whether the so-called scientific worldview is exhaustive in the sense that it excludes both the possibility of and the need for an extra-scientific worldview. From a scriptural standpoint, it would appear that a scientific worldview is, in the end, partial in character, and that, while a God-oriented worldview is both generative of and inclusive of a scientific worldview, the converse is not true. Another relevant question is this: Talk of a personal God ultimately is talk of a God of many attributes, these attributes having a direct bearing on the life and conduct of human beings. Above all, it is talk of an ethical God that demands ethical behavior of human beings. Because science is ethically neutral, the conjunction of a scripture-based ethical human behavior with a so-called scientific worldview should fall within the realm of possibility. The precise details of such a conjunction, however, must be worked out from a religious viewpoint.

2. What is the relationship between religious and scientific language? There is no question that religion and science speak two different languages. The language of scripture, which we may here take to represent the language of religion, cannot be employed in carrying out chemical experiments, and scripture's reference to the existence of, for example, seven heavens, would ring no bells with a scholar of science. The attempt to establish common points between the two languages would, accordingly, seem futile. But while no direct, language-to-language relationship can be established between science and scripture, such a relationship between the two can probably be established with reference to something that stands outside both scripture and science—namely, human experience, which gives rise to and justifies and validates both scientific and religious language just as it gives rise to and justifies and validates, for example, poetic language. The question to investigate,

then, is whether the languages of religion and science cater to certain distinct, if equally valid, human needs and in doing so justify their existence. A no less important question is whether the claims to truth made in the two languages could at times come into conflict, and whether a framework or mechanism exists or can be created for resolving such a conflict, should it arise.

3. Do all the scriptural texts in question bear equally forcefully on the science–religion relationship? That does not appear to be the case. Some of the texts seem to have a greater appeal for the "scientific imagination," such as 21:30: "We made every living thing from water"; or 10:5, which makes a nuanced reference to the difference between the light of the sun and the light of the moon: "It is He who made the sun a shining radiance [ḍiyā'] and the moon a light [nūr]"; or 13:2: "It is God who raised up the heavens with no visible supports." There are also verses that refer to phenomenal reality but seek to derive from it lessons that are more suggested than stated, such as 2:164, which points to a number of natural phenomena, concluding with the observations that "there are signs in all these for those who use their minds." How can verses that are relatively more intriguing for a scientific mind be related to those with a heavy theological or dogmatic content? Is it possible to establish a hierarchy of Qur'ānic verses bearing on the religion–science issue with a view to generating a hermeneutic employable in a religion–science discourse?

4. Perhaps from a religious viewpoint the ultimate challenge would be to inquire into the possibility of accommodating a scientific outlook as a subset of the religious outlook. At the highest level, religion takes as its province the whole of reality while science must be content to deal with segments or compartments of reality and must, furthermore, remain silent on the question of valuation of reality, whether taken as a whole or in parts. Any attempt to subsume a scientific outlook under a religious outlook, however, must ensure the presence of coherence and continuity between the two types of outlook.

Classical Christian Texts

Basil of Caesarea: *Hexaemeron*

Homily I

2. "In the beginning God created the heaven and the earth." I stop struck
with admiration at this thought. What shall I first say? Where shall I
begin my story? Shall I show forth the vanity of the Gentiles? Shall I
exalt the truth of our faith? The philosophers of Greece have made
much ado to explain nature, and not one of their systems has remained
firm and unshaken, each being overturned by its successor. It is vain to
refute them; they are sufficient in themselves to destroy one another.
Those who were too ignorant to rise to a knowledge of a God, could
not allow that an intelligent cause presided at the birth of the Universe;
a primary error that involved them in sad consequences. Some had
recourse to material principles and attributed the origin of the Universe
to the elements of the world. Others imagined that atoms, and indivisi-
ble bodies, molecules and ducts, form, by their union, the nature of the
visible world. Atoms reuniting or separating produce births and deaths
and the most durable bodies only owe their consistency to the strength
of their mutual adhesion: a true spider's web woven by these writers
who give to heaven, to earth, and to sea so weak an origin and so little
consistency! It is because they knew not how to say "In the beginning
God created the heaven and the earth." Deceived by their inherent
atheism it appeared to them that nothing governed or ruled the universe, and that all was given up to chance. To guard us against this
error the writer on the creation, from the very first words, enlightens
our understanding with the name of God; "In the beginning God
created." . . .

3. . . . Of what use then are geometry—the calculations of arithmetic—the
study of solids and far-famed astronomy, this laborious vanity, if those

74

who pursue them imagine that this visible world is co-eternal with the Creator of all things, with God Himself; if they attribute to this limited world, which has a material body, the same glory as to the incomprehensible and invisible nature; if they cannot conceive that a whole, of which the parts are subject to corruption and change, must of necessity end by itself submitting to the fate of its parts? But they have become "vain in their imaginations and their foolish heart was darkened. Professing themselves to be wise, they became fools" [Rom 1:21–22]. Some have affirmed that heaven co-exists with God from all eternity; others that it is God Himself without beginning or end, and the cause of the particular arrangement of all things.

4. One day, doubtless, their terrible condemnation will be the greater for all this worldly wisdom, since, seeing so clearly into vain sciences, they have wilfully shut their eyes to the knowledge of the truth. These men who measure the distances of the stars and describe them, both those of the North, always shining brilliantly in our view, and those of the southern pole visible to the inhabitants of the South, but unknown to us; who divide the Northern zone and the circle of the Zodiac into an infinity of parts, who observe with exactitude the course of the stars, their fixed places, their declensions, their return and the time that each takes to make its revolution; these men, I say, have discovered all except one thing: the fact that God is the Creator of the universe, and the just Judge who rewards all the actions of life according to their merit.[1]

Gregory of Nyssa: *On the Making of Man*

Ch. VIII

3. Let us . . . consider . . . why the growth of things that spring from the earth takes precedence, and the irrational animals come next, and then, after the making of these, comes man: for it may be that we learn from these facts not only the obvious thought, that grass appeared to the Creator useful for the sake of the animals, while the animals were made because of man, and that for this reason, before the animals there was made their food, and before man that which was to minister to human life.

4. But it seems to me that by these facts Moses reveals a hidden doctrine, and secretly delivers that wisdom concerning the soul, of which the learning that is without had indeed some imagination, but no clear comprehension. His discourse then hereby teaches us that the power of life and soul may be considered in three divisions. For one is only a power of growth and nutrition supplying what is suitable for the support of the bodies that are nourished, which is called the vegetative soul, and is to be seen in plants; for we may perceive in growing plants a certain vital power destitute of sense; and there is another form of life besides this, which, while it includes the form above mentioned, is also possessed in addition of the power of management according to sense; and this is to be found in the nature of the irrational animals: for they are not only the subjects of nourishment and growth, but also have the activity of sense and perception. But perfect bodily life is seen in the rational (I mean the human) nature, which both is nourished and endowed with sense, and also partakes of reason and is ordered by mind. . . .

7. If, therefore, Scripture tells us that man was made last, after every animate thing, the lawgiver [Moses] is doing nothing else than declaring to us the doctrine of the soul, considering that what is perfect comes last, according to a certain necessary sequence in the order of things: for in the rational are included the others also, while in the sensitive there also surely exists the vegetative form, and that again is conceived only in connection with what is material: thus we may suppose that nature makes an ascent as it were by steps—I mean the various properties of life—from the lower to the perfect form.

Ch. XXIX

2. For as our nature is conceived as twofold, according to the apostolic teaching, made up of the visible man and the hidden man, if the one came first and the other supervened, the power of Him that made us will be shown to be in some way imperfect, as not being completely sufficient for the whole task at once, but dividing the work, and busying itself with each of the halves in turn.

3. But just as we say that in wheat, or in any other grain, the whole form of the plant is potentially included—the leaves, the stalk, the joints, the grain, the beard—and do not say in our account of its nature that any

of these things has pre-existence, or comes into being before the others, but that the power abiding in the seed is manifested in a certain natural order, not by any means that another nature is infused into it—in the same way we suppose the human germ to possess the potentiality of its nature, sown with it at the first start of its existence, and that it is unfolded and manifested by a natural sequence as it proceeds to its perfect state, not employing anything external to itself as a stepping-stone to perfection, but itself advancing its own self in due course to the perfect state; so that it is not true to say either that the soul exists before the body, or that the body exists without the soul, but that there is one beginning of both, which according to the heavenly view was laid as their foundation in the original will of God; according to the other, came into existence on the occasion of generation.

4. For as we cannot discern the articulation of the limbs in that which is implanted for the conception of the body before it begins to take form, so neither is it possible to perceive in the same the properties of the soul before they advance to operation; and just as no one would doubt that the thing so implanted is fashioned into the different varieties of limbs and interior organs, not by the importation of any other power from without, but by the power which resides in it transforming it to this manifestation of energy,—so also we may by like reasoning equally suppose in the case of the soul that even if it is not visibly recognized by any manifestations of activity it none the less is there; for even the form of the future man is there potentially, but is concealed because it is not possible that it should be made visible before the necessary sequence of events allows it; so also the soul is there, even though it is not visible, and will be manifested by means of its own proper and natural operation, as it advances concurrently with the bodily growth.[2]

Augustine: *The Literal Meaning of Genesis*

Usually, even a non-Christian knows something about the earth, the heavens, and the other elements of this world, about the motion and orbit of the stars and even their size and relative positions, about the predictable eclipses of the sun and moon, the cycles of the years and the season, about the kinds of animals, shrubs, stones, and so forth, and this knowledge he holds to as being certain from reason and experience. Now, it is a disgraceful and dangerous thing for an infidel to hear a Christian, presumably giving the meaning of Holy Scripture, talking nonsense on these topics; and we should take all means to prevent such an embarrassing situation, in which people show up vast ignorance in a Christian and laugh it to scorn. The shame is not so much that an ignorant individual is derided, but that people outside the household of the faith think our sacred writers held such opinions, and, to the great loss of those for whose salvation we toil, the writers of our Scripture are criticized and rejected as unlearned men. (1.19.39)[3]

For through Wisdom all things were made, and the motion we now see in creatures, measured by the lapse of time, as each one fulfils its proper function, comes to creatures from those causal reasons implanted in them, which God scattered as seeds at the moment of creation when *He spoke and they were made, He commanded and they were created*. (4.33.51)[4]

Let us, then, consider the beauty of any tree in its trunk, branches, leaves, and fruit. This tree surely did not spring forth suddenly in this size and form, but rather went through a process of growth with which we are familiar. For it sprouted forth from a root which a germ or bud first planted in the earth, and from that source the tree took its shape as it developed with all its parts. Furthermore, the germ was from a seed, and therefore in the seed all those parts existed primordially, not in the dimensions of bodily mass but as a force and causal power. The bodily mass was built up by an accumulation of earth and moisture. But there exists in the tiny grain that power more wonderful and excellent by which moisture was mingled with earth forming a matter capable of being changed into wood, into spreading branches, into green leaves of appropriate shape, into beautiful and luxurious fruits, with all parts developed into a well-ordered whole. For what comes forth from that tree or hangs upon it that was not taken or drawn from a hidden treasure in the seed? . . .

In the seed, then, there was invisibly present all that would develop in time to a tree. And in this same way we must picture the world, when God made all things together, as having had all things together which were made in it and with it when day was made. This includes not only heaven with sun, moon, and stars, whose splendor remains unchanged as they move in a circular motion; and earth and the deep waters, which are in almost unceasing motion, and which, placed below the sky, make up the lowest part of the world; but it includes also the beings which water and earth produced in potency and in their causes before they came forth in the course of time as they have become known to us in the works which God even now produces . . .

God, then, creates no new creatures, but He directs and rules by His governance of the world all the things He made together, and thus He works without ceasing, resting and working at the same time, as I have already explained. (5.23.44–46)[5]

For in that first creation of the world, when God created all things simultaneously, He created man in the sense that he made the man who was to be, that is, the causal principle of man to be created, not the actuality of man already created. (6.9.16)[6]

Now, if the original works of God, when he created all things simultaneously, were not perfect according to the limits of their nature, no doubt there would later be added the perfections needed to complete their being; and thus the perfection of the world is made up of what we might call two halves. As they are like parts of a whole, the total universe, whose parts they are, is completed by their union. Moreover, if these creatures attained perfection in the sense that they are perfected when they are brought forth individually, each at its own time, in their visible form and reality, it is surely true that either nothing would come from them later as time unfolds, or God would unceasingly produce from them the effects which in due time have their origin in them.

But these works in a certain sense are already perfected, and in another sense they are just begun. They were made by God, when in the beginning he made the world and created simultaneously all things to be made in the ages to follow. They are perfected because in their proper natures by which they fulfil their role in time they have nothing that was not present in them as made in its causes. They are just begun, however, since in them are seeds, as it were, of future perfections to be put forth from their hidden state and made manifest during the ages at the appropriate time. (6.11.18)[7]

The ordinary course of nature in the whole of creation has certain natural laws. . . . The elements of the physical world also have a fixed power and quality determining for each thing what it can do or not do and what can be done or not done with it. From these elements all things which come to be in due time have their origin and development as well as their end and dissolution according to their kind. Thus, a bean does not come from a grain of wheat nor wheat from a bean, and a man does not come from a beast nor a beast from a man.

Over this whole movement and course of nature there is the power of the Creator, who is able to do in all creatures something other than what the seminal reasons would bring about, but not something that He himself had not originally made possible to be done by Him in them. For He is all-powerful not by arbitrary power but by the strength of wisdom, and in the course of time He does with each thing what He originally has made possible in it. (9.17.32)[8]

Notes

1. Christian Classics Ethereal Library, accessed September 8, 2011, www.ccel.org/ccel/schaff/npnf208.viii.ii.html.

2. Christian Classics Ethereal Library, accessed September 8, 2011, www.ccel.org/ccel/schaff/npnf205.x.ii.ii.i.html.

3. St. Augustine, *The Literal Meaning of Genesis* (New York: Paulist Press, 1982), vol. 1, 42–43.

4. Ibid., 141. Emphasis in original.

5. Ibid., 174–76.

6. Ibid., 179.

7. Ibid., 190–91.

8. Ibid., vol. 2, 92–93.

Commentary

Science and Religion in the Classical Christian Tradition

Emmanuel Clapsis

General Remarks

As the Christian Church expanded its mission to the Hellenistic world, it had to develop the language and system of thought necessary to make Christianity comprehensible to those who did not operate within a Judaic frame of mind. Those who had studied Greek philosophy and science and desired to give Christian orientation to their philosophical thinking and rationality undertook this task. While these thinkers repudiated the theological implications of some Hellenistic cosmologies, at the same time they acknowledged elements of truth in them that provided either support or illustrations for an expanded and coherent interpretation of the Christian cosmogony.

The most notable attitudes in Christian tradition toward the relationship between faith and science had already emerged in the second and third centuries. Because the faith of the Church about the origins, the nature, and the future of the world was primarily informed by its interpretations of God's revelation, some thought that speculation, no matter how deeply concerned with the quest for truth, could add nothing to what God had revealed. They stressed exclusively the novelty of Christianity and denigrated pagan philosophy. Others suggested that philosophers had borrowed whatever was true and valuable in their thinking about the world from scripture.

St. Justin Martyr (ca. 100–ca. 165) provides a significant pattern of integrating faith with philosophical and scientific knowledge. He argued that whatever element of truth could be found in philosophical thought was the residue of a revelation. Instead of saying that all truth came from revelation, he admitted that human reason had access to truth even though, being human, it often fell into error. Through the Stoic notion of *logos spermatikos*, the "seminal word," Justin acknowledged that the universe was wholly permeated by a cosmic reason, logos. This logos, disseminated among all men at all times, was a kind of fragmentary anticipation of and participation in the whole truth, which was revealed in the Logos made flesh.

St. Irenaeus (ca. 130–ca. 200), writing a generation after Justin, presents a different view on how theology relates to philosophical thought. He was convinced that human thinking, valuable and truthful though it may be, cannot know God and his dispensation. For Irenaeus, salvation was only to be attained through faith in what God had revealed, and, more important still, in what he had done. Human reason and divine revelation were, so to speak, in different dimensions. Man's intellectual quest, no matter how far-reaching, can never become God's own self-communication in revelation, nor can it be a substitute for it. According to Irenaeus, the relationship within the Christian mind of human thought and faith can only be grounded on complete, unreserved, and unconditional acceptance of revelation and of its preeminence over human reasoning and philosophical speculation. Once that is assured, total freedom is granted to Christian thought to draw on any philosophical or other kind of insight to deepen its understanding of what it believes by faith.

The three classical texts to be discussed here were written by St. Basil of Caesarea (ca. 330–379); his brother, St. Gregory of Nyssa (ca. 335–394); and St. Augustine of Hippo (354–430). They reflect mostly the Irenaean view (faith seeking understanding) and in some instances, the view of Justin. They illustrate the patristic pattern of relating revelation to demonstrative reason and experience. The narrative of Christian cosmogony is primarily characterized by faithfulness to the basic precepts of the biblical story and extensive use of the scientific and philosophical reasoning of Hellenistic thought.

These passages are representative samples of how three major Christian theologians related their theology of Creation to philosophical and scientific reasoning. While Basil and Gregory have shaped the ethos and theology of Eastern Christianity, Augustine is considered among the most influential representative thinkers of Western Christianity. All three belong to the undivided tradition of the Christian church. All were men of faith with formal training in philosophy and science. For their time, they make skillful use of their philosophical and scientific knowledge to illustrate the dynamic nature of the created world. It is their mission as pastors and theologians to give a credible and intelligible account of their faith for God's glory.

The three texts were written for different purposes. The text from Basil is from a Lenten sermon that aims to build up and strengthen the faith of his congregation in God as the Creator of the world *ex nihilo*. The passage from Gregory comes from one of the earliest systematic and reflective treatises on Christian anthropology. The passage from Augustine is from his exegetical commentary on Genesis, written in light of the best philosophical and scientific knowledge of his time.

St. Basil: *Hexaemeron*

Basil was one of the most brilliant ecclesiastical orators of antiquity. His homilies on the *Hexaemeron*, the narrative of the "Six Days" of Creation in Genesis 1:1–26, are Lenten sermons delivered before AD 370. His purpose was to give his congregation a Christian understanding of cosmogony that would lead them to recognize God as the Creator of the universe. Insights from philosophy and natural science are used in these homilies to illustrate the beauty and complexity of the world in order to affirm faith in God's providence and wisdom. He moves from physics that discussed the origins, the becoming and the future of the universe, to the One who "created the heaven and the Earth" (section 2).

Basil judged all the cosmologies known to him as mistaken in their inability to acknowledge God as the Creator of the universe, their failure to recognize that "an intelligent cause presided at the birth of the Universe" (section 2). This led them to the belief "that nothing governed or rule the universe, and that all was given up to chance" (section 2). Basil presents the classical Christian view of the radical distinction between God and the world: the universe is not coeternal with God. The world created by the will of the benevolent God is essentially good and a beautiful and purposeful artifact. It is dynamic and developmental in nature, "subject to corruption and change" (section 3). The universe as created artifact, bounded by time, does not have the same glory as the uncreated and eternal God.

Basil urges his congregation not to take seriously the different systems of "the philosophers of Greece" (section 2) on account of their multiplicity and the fact that they contradict one another, in addition to their inability to acknowledge "that an intelligent cause presided at the birth of the Universe." In discussing the science of astronomy, Basil acknowledges the veracity of its observations and concedes that astronomers "have discovered all except one thing"—the fact that God is the Creator of the world (section 4). For Basil, scientific discoveries and explanations of the workings of nature are welcomed as illustrations or elucidations of basic precepts of the biblical story, most especially that the world has been created by God and is dependent upon him for its sustenance.

St. Gregory of Nyssa: *De hominis opificio*

In his last homily on the *Hexaemeron* Basil announced that he would give a homily on man as the image of God. It seems that he never delivered it, and Gregory of Nyssa composed his *De hominis opificio* shortly after Basil's death (379) with the special purpose of completing his brother's work on the *Hexaemeron*. *De hominis opificio* is not a homily delivered for the edification of the faithful but rather a reflective treatise intending to contribute toward the development of a comprehensive Christian anthropology.

At the time of St. Gregory, there was awareness in the church of the need to consider human beings as part of the universe. For many thinkers (Plato, Philo, and Origen), the universe was divided into two orders, the spiritual or rational and the material or irrational. Gregory incorporates this dichotomy into his understanding of human beings. God, having created two worlds, the suprasensible and the sensible, finally created man and woman in order to be a link between these two worlds. To affect this link and unify the entire creation, it was necessary that human beings would share in these two worlds and be a mixture or combination of both. This unity of the material and the spiritual is not only reflected in the unity of body and soul but also in the very constitution of the soul. Although Gregory insisted on the simple, uncompounded nature and the indivisibility of the soul, he identified in the soul three inseparable powers or faculties: the rational, the sensitive, and the vegetative.

Reflecting on the sequence of the biblical story of Creation, Gregory writes that Moses "reveals a hidden doctrine, and secretly delivers that wisdom concerning the soul, of which the learning that is without had indeed some imagination, but no clear comprehension" (VIII.4). He acknowledges that some truth about the soul and its constitution can be found in those who do not share the fullness of God's revelation. For Gregory, the origins of the soul are incomprehensible since scripture does not discuss the matter. Thus with the absence of scriptural evidence for or against any theory respecting the origin of the soul, Gregory is free to turn to what philosophy had to say on this matter.

Gregory rejects belief in the preexistence of the soul and its transmigration and affirms the simultaneous beginning of both soul and body, which have their origins in God's will. The simultaneous beginning of body and soul substantiates the unity of human nature as well as the dignity, the sanctity, and the essential goodness of both body and soul as constitutive and inseparable aspects of a human being. In discussing the unity of the body and soul and the dynamic development of human beings, Gregory uses an observation from life:

> But just as we say that in wheat, or in any other grain, the whole form of the plant is potentially included—the leaves, the stalk, the joints, the grain, the beard—and do not say in our account of its nature that any of these things has pre-existence, or comes into being before the others, but the power abiding in the seed is manifested in a certain natural order . . . in the same way we suppose the human germ to possess the potentiality of its nature, sown with it at the first start of its existence, and that it is unfolded and manifested by a natural sequence as it proceeds to its perfect state . . . (XXIX.3)

Here Gregory seems to lean heavily on Aristotle, in whose view the soul is from the beginning in the visible (φαινόμενον) but cannot be seen. The soul will be seen, however, through the activity (ενέργεια) that is particular to it, and which advances along with the growth of the body. Throughout the process of growth the soul is the determining principle (αρχή) or cause (αφορμή) in living beings.

In his discussion of the constitution of the soul and its relation to the body, Gregory provides an admirable expansion of theological imagination that creatively advances Christian anthropology. While the biblical story of Creation is the basis of his reflection, he does not hesitate to use insights, linguistic and conceptual, from Hellenistic philosophy to communicate in an intelligible way the dynamic nature of humanity.

As we have seen, Basil defended those elements of the Christian narrative of Creation that he thought were at risk of being misinterpreted by the advances of the scientific and philosophical theories of his time. Gregory, in contrast, used elements from Hellenistic philosophies in order to affirm the dynamic nature of human life and affirm that human beings are at the same time spiritual and material beings. Later, Augustine found it necessary to write his commentary on Genesis to safeguard the Christian narrative of Creation from its misinterpretation not necessarily by the "philosophers of Greece" but by believers who were talking nonsense on this matter, thus damaging the Church's salvific ministry.

St. Augustine of Hippo: *The Literal Meaning of Genesis*

St. Augustine seems to equal Gregory in his appreciation and use of natural philosophy. His works reveal a man broadly educated in the full range of the liberal arts. He frequently acknowledges the usefulness of natural knowledge for the elucidation of Christian doctrine and the exegesis of scripture. Non-Christians were capable of understanding the world as it really is, and Christians, according to Augustine, should not dismiss their views outright or misrepresent the faith by "talking nonsense on these topics" (1.19.39). For Augustine, those who attempt to interpret the biblical story of Creation without taking into account what can be learned from reason and experience misrepresent the faith of the church.

In 415 Augustine wrote *De Genesi ad Litteram* (*The Literal Meaning of Genesis*), in which he attempts to weave the best of the scientific knowledge of his day into his interpretation of the Genesis narrative. Even though his work is titled *The Literal Meaning of Genesis*, he does not read Genesis 1 in the same "literal" way as modern creationists. He claims that Creation is an instantaneous event rather than an event spread out over six literal days. The metaphorical interpretation that he gives to some biblical passages raises a difficult hermeneutical problem: How is one to decide when a biblical expression is metaphorical without compromising the absolute authority of the literal meaning of God's word?

The interweaving of theology with natural knowledge is reflected in his doctrine of *rationes seminales* or "seedlike principles" ("seminal reasons," in the translation included in this volume). The stoic notion that nature contains germs or seedlike principles that direct and determine its subsequent unfolding became the basis of his understanding that God created all things in the beginning, some actually and some potentially—the latter as seedlike principles, which later developed into mature creatures, much as a seed develops into a mature plant. Augustine maintains that God's creative activity is not actually completed in the beginning but some aspects of the created world were subject to development as can be easily observed.

This doctrine of seedlike principles acknowledges that God has bestowed on nature some degree of rational structure that guides its development. "The elements of the physical world also have a fixed power and quality determining for each thing what it can do or not do and what can be done or not done with it" (9.17.32). For Augustine, there is a kind of double causation in the created world: on the one hand, things change and develop according to the nature that God has given them; on the other hand, God is "able to do in all creatures something other than what the seminal reasons would bring about, but not something that He himself had not originally made possible to be done by Him in them" (9.17.32).

For Further Reflection

1. The conversation between theology and science enhances the understanding of reality through observations, insights, and critique that both theology and science address to one another. The conversation itself does not deny the irreducible differences that allow theology and science to be distinct from each other. Resisting all forms of religious and scientific reductionism, are we ready to acknowledge and respect the irresolvable and inconclusive differences that remind both science and theology that the universe is a much more complex and open reality than our systems of thought and tradition may allow?

2. Are scientific discoveries and explanations of nature simply welcome elucidations of the Christian narrative of Creation?

3. How do we relate the rational structure of nature and divinely granted purposeful existence with human freedom and with God's grace and absolute freedom?

4. In the absence of scriptural and historical insights or guidance on some aspects of the working of nature, do we have the liberty to use the wisdom of science to articulate our Christian understanding of reality or even to change some moral positions that faith communities have developed based on inaccurate descriptions of how natural things are?

Classical Islamic Texts

Al-Ghazālī: *al-Munqidh min al-ḍalāl* (Deliverance from Error)

AFTER I HAD DONE WITH THEOLOGY I started on philosophy. I was convinced that a man cannot grasp what is defective in any of the sciences unless he has so complete a grasp of the science in question that he equals its most learned exponents in the appreciation of its fundamental principles, and even goes beyond and surpasses them, probing into some of the tangles and profundities which the very professors of the science have neglected. Then and only then is it possible that what he has to assert about its defects is true.

So far as I could see none of the doctors of Islam had devoted thought and attention to philosophy. In their writings none of the theologians engaged in polemic against the philosophers, apart from obscure and scattered utterances so plainly erroneous and inconsistent that no person of ordinary intelligence would be likely to be deceived, far less one versed in the sciences.

I realized that to refute a system before understanding it and becoming acquainted with its depths is to act blindly. I therefore set out in all earnestness to acquire a knowledge of philosophy from books, by private study without the help of an instructor. I made progress towards this aim during my hours of free time after teaching in the religious sciences and writing, for at this period I was burdened with the teaching and instruction of three hundred students in Baghdad. By my solitary reading during the hours thus snatched God brought me in less than two years to a complete understanding of the sciences of the philosophers. Thereafter I continued to reflect assiduously for nearly a year on what I had assimilated, going over it in my mind again and again and probing its tangled depths, until I comprehended surely and certainly how far it was deceitful and confusing and how far true and a representation of reality.

Hear now an account of this discipline and of the achievement of the sciences it comprises. There are various schools of philosophers, I perceived, and their sciences are divided into various branches; but throughout their numerous schools they suffer from the defect of being infidels and irreligious men, even although of the different groups of philosophers—older and most ancient, earlier and more recent—some are much closer to the truth than others.

A. *The schools of philosophers, and how the defect of unbelief affects them all.*

The many philosophical sects and systems constitute three main groups: the Materialists (*Dahrīyūn*), the Naturalists (*Ṭabī'īyūn*), and the Theists (*Ilāhīyūn*).

The first group, the *Materialists*, are among the earliest philosophers. They deny the Creator and Disposer of the world, omniscient and omnipotent, and consider that the world has everlastingly existed just as it is, of itself and without a creator, and that everlastingly animals have come from seed and seed from animals; thus it was and thus it ever will be. These are the Zanadiqah or irreligious people.

The second group, the *Naturalists*, are a body of philosophers who have engaged in manifold researches into the world of nature and the marvels of animals and plants and have expended much effort in the science of dissecting the organs of animals. They see there sufficient of the wonders of God's creation and the inventions of His wisdom to compel them to acknowledge a wise Creator Who is aware of the aims and purposes of things. No one can make a careful study of anatomy and the wonderful uses of the members and organs without attaining to the necessary knowledge that there is a perfection in the order which the framer gave to the animal frame, and especially to that of man.

Yet these philosophers, immersed in their researches into nature, take the view that the equal balance of the temperament has great influence in constituting the powers of animals. They hold that even the intellectual power in man is dependent on the temperament, so that as the temperament is corrupted intellect also is corrupted and ceases to exist. Further, when a thing ceases to exist, it is unthinkable in their opinion that the non-existent should return to existence. Thus it is their view that the soul dies and does not return to life, and they deny the future life—heaven, hell, resurrection and judgement; there does not remain, they hold, any reward for obedience or any punishment for sin. With the curb removed they give way to a bestial indulgence of their appetites.

These are also irreligious, for the basis of faith is faith in God, and in the Last Day, and these, though believing in God and His attributes, deny the Last Day.

The third group, the *Theists*, are the more modern philosophers and include Socrates, his pupil Plato, and the latter's pupil Aristotle. It was Aristotle who systematized logic for them and organized the sciences, securing a higher degree of accuracy and bringing them to maturity.

The Theists in general attacked the two previous groups, the Materialists and the Naturalists, and exposed their defects so effectively that others were relieved of the task. "And God relieved the believers of fighting" (Q. 33, 25) through their mutual combat. Aristotle, moreover, attacked his predecessors among the Theistic philosophers, especially Plato and Socrates, and went so far in his criticisms that he separated himself from them all. Yet he too retained a residue of their unbelief and heresy from which he did not manage to free himself. We must therefore reckon as unbelievers both these philosophers themselves and their followers among the Islamic philosophers, such as Ibn Sīnā, al-Fārābī and others; in transmitting the philosophy of Aristotle, however, none of the Islamic philosophers has accomplished anything comparable to the achievements of the two men named. The translations of others are marked by disorder and confusion, which so perplex the understanding of the student that he fails to comprehend; and if a thing is not comprehended, how can it be either refuted or accepted?

All that, in our view, genuinely is part of the philosophy of Aristotle, as these men have transmitted it, falls under three heads: (1) what must be counted as unbelief; (2) what must be counted as heresy; (3) what is not to be denied at all. Let us proceed, then, to the details.

B. The Various Philosophical Sciences. For our present purpose the philosophical sciences are six in number: mathematics, logic, natural science, theology, politics, ethics.

1. MATHEMATICS. This embraces arithmetic, plane geometry, and solid geometry. None of its results are connected with religious matters, either to deny or to affirm them. They are matters of demonstration, which it is impossible to deny once they have been understood and apprehended. Nevertheless, there are two drawbacks which arise from mathematics.

(a) The first is that every student of mathematics admires its precision and the clarity of its demonstrations. This leads him to believe in the philosophers and to think that all their sciences resemble this one in clarity and demonstrative cogency. Further, he has already heard the accounts on everyone's lips of their unbelief, their denial of God's attributes, and their contempt for revealed truth; he becomes an unbeliever merely by accepting them as authorities (*bi'l-taqlīd al-maḥḍ*), and says to himself, "If religion were true, it would not have escaped the notice of these men since they are so precise in this science." Thus, after becoming acquainted by hearsay with their unbelief and denial of religion, he draws the conclusion that the truth is the denial and rejection of religion. How many have I seen who err from the truth because of this high opinion of the philosophers and without any other basis!

Against them one may argue: "The man who excels in one art does not necessarily excel in every art. It is not necessary that the man who excels in law and theology should excel in medicine, nor that the man who is ignorant of intellectual speculations should be ignorant of grammar. Rather, every art has people who have obtained excellence and preeminence in it, even though stupidity and ignorance may characterize them in other arts. The arguments in elementary matters of mathematics are demonstrative, whereas those in theology (or metaphysics) are based on conjecture. This point is familiar only to those who have studied the matter deeply for themselves."

If such a person is fixed in this belief which he has chosen out of respect for authority (*taqlīd*), he is not moved by this argument but is carried by strength of passion, love of vanity, and the desire to be thought clever to persist in his good opinion of the philosophers with regard to all the sciences.

This is a great drawback, and because of it those who devote themselves eagerly to the mathematical sciences ought to be restrained. Even if their subject matter is not relevant to religion, yet, since they belong to the foundations of the philosophical sciences, the student is infected with the evil and corruption of the philosophers. Few there are who devote themselves to this study without being stripped of religion and having the bridle of godly fear removed from their heads.

(b) The second drawback arises from the man who is loyal to Islam but ignorant. He thinks that religion must be defended by rejecting every science connected with the philosophers, and so rejects all their sciences and accuses them of ignorance therein. He even rejects their theory of the eclipse of sun and moon, considering that what they say is contrary to revelation. When that view is thus attacked, someone hears who has knowledge of such matters by apodeictic demonstration. He does not doubt his demonstration, but, believing that Islam is based on ignorance and the denial of apodeictic proof, grows in love for philosophy and hatred for Islam.

A grievous crime indeed against religion has been committed by the man who imagines that Islam is defended by the denial of the mathematical sciences, seeing that there is nothing in revealed truth opposed to these sciences by way of either negation or affirmation, and nothing in these sciences opposed to the truths of religion. Muḥammad (peace be upon him) said, "The sun and the moon are two of the signs of God; they are not eclipsed for anyone's death nor for his life; if you see such an event, take refuge in the recollection of God (most high) and in prayer." There is nothing here obliging us to deny the science of arithmetic which informs us specifically of the orbits of sun and moon, and their conjunction and opposition. (The further saying of Muḥammad (peace be upon him), "When God manifests Himself to a thing, it submits to Him," is an addition which does not occur at all in the collections of sound Traditions.)

This is the character of mathematics and its drawbacks.

2. LOGIC. Nothing in logic is relevant to religion by way of denial or affirmation. Logic is the study of the methods of demonstration and of forming syllogisms, of the conditions for the premises of proofs, of the manner of combining the premises, of the conditions for sound definition and the manner of ordering it. Knowledge comprises (a) the concept (*taṣawwur*), which is apprehended by definition, and (b) the assertion or judgement (*taṣdīq*), which is apprehended by proof. There is nothing here which requires to be denied. Matters of this kind are actually mentioned by the theologians and speculative thinkers in connection with the topic of demonstrations. The philosophers differ from these only in the expressions and technical terms they employ and in their greater elaboration of the explanations and classifications. An example of this is their proposition, "If it is true that all A is B, then it follows that some B is A," that is, "If it is true that all men are animals, then it follows that some animals are men." They express this by saying that "the universal *affirmative* proposition has as its converse a particular affirmative proposition." What connection has this with the essentials of religion, that it should be denied or rejected? If such a denial is made, the only effect upon the logicians is to impair their belief in the intelligence of the man who made the denial

and, what is worse, in his religion, inasmuch as he considers that it rests on such denials.

Moreover, there is a type of mistake into which students of logic are liable to fall. They draw up a list of the conditions to be fulfilled by demonstration, which are known without fail to produce certainty. When, however, they come at length to treat of religious questions, not merely are they unable to satisfy these conditions, but they admit an extreme degree of relaxation (sc. of their standards of proof). Frequently, too, the student who admires logic and sees its clarity, imagines that the infidel doctrines attributed to the philosophers are supported by similar demonstrations, and hastens into unbelief before reaching the theological (or metaphysical) sciences. Thus this drawback too leads to unbelief.

3. NATURAL SCIENCE OR PHYSICS. This is the investigation of the sphere of the heavens together with the heavenly bodies, and of what is beneath the heavens, both simple bodies like water, air, earth, fire, and composite bodies like animals, plants and minerals, and also of the causes of their changes, transformations and combinations. This is similar to the investigation by medicine of the human body with its principal and subordinate organs, and of the causes of the changes of temperament. Just as it is not a condition of religion to reject medical science, so likewise the rejection of natural science is not one of its conditions, except with regard to particular points which I enumerate in my book, *The Incoherence of the Philosophers.* Any other points on which a different view has to be taken from the philosophers are shown by reflection to be implied in those mentioned. The basis of all these objections is the recognition that nature is in subjection to God most high, not acting of itself but serving as an instrument in the hands of its Creator. Sun and moon, stars and elements, are in subjection to His command. There is none of them whose activity is produced by or proceeds from its own essence.

4. THEOLOGY OR METAPHYSICS. Here occur most of the errors of the philosophers. They are unable to satisfy the conditions of proof they lay down in logic, and consequently differ much from one another here. The views of Aristotle, as expounded by al-Fārābī and Ibn Sīnā, are close to those of the Islamic writers. All their errors are comprised under twenty heads, on three of which they must be reckoned infidels and on seventeen heretics. It was to show the falsity of their views on these twenty points that I composed

The Incoherence of the Philosophers. The three points in which they differ from all the Muslims are as follows:

(a) They say that for bodies there is no resurrection; it is bare spirits which are rewarded or punished; and the rewards and punishments are spiritual, not bodily. They certainly speak truth in affirming the spiritual ones, since these do exist as well; but they speak falsely in denying the bodily ones and in their pronouncements disbelieve the Divine law.

(b) They say that God knows universals but not particulars. This too is plain unbelief. The truth is that "there does not escape Him the weight of an atom in the heavens or in the earth" (Q. 34, 3).

(c) They say that the world is everlasting, without beginning or end. But no Muslim has adopted any such view on this question.

On the further points—their denial of the attributes of God, their doctrine that God knows by His essence and not by a knowledge which is over and above His essence, and the like—their position approximates to that of the Mu'tazilah; and the Mu'tazilah must not be accounted infidels because of such matters. In my book, *The Decisive Criterion for Distinguishing Islam from Heresy,* I have presented the grounds for regarding as corrupt the opinion of those who hastily pronounce a man an infidel if he deviates from their own system of doctrine.[1]

Ibn Rushd: *Tahāfut al-tahāfut* (The Incoherence of the Incoherence)

The title of this work by Ibn Rushd (Averroes) refers to al-Ghazālī's work The Incoherence of the Philosophers. *The passage that follows is from a section on the Natural Sciences; here Ibn Rushd critiques al-Ghazālī's denial that there is a necessary relationship between cause and effect. He first quotes al-Ghazālī at length and then gives his response.*

Ghazali says:

According to us the connexion between what is usually believed to be a cause and what is believed to be an effect is not a necessary connexion; each of two things has its own individuality and is not the other, and neither the affirmation nor the negation, neither the existence nor the non-existence of the one is implied in the affirmation, negation, existence, and non-existence of the other—e.g., the satisfaction of thirst does not imply drinking, nor satiety eating, nor burning contact with fire, nor light sunrise, nor decapitation death, nor recovery the drinking of medicine, nor evacuation the taking of a purgative, and so on for all the empirical connexions existing in medicine, astronomy, the sciences, and the crafts. For the connexion in these things is based on a prior power of God to create them in a successive order, though not because this connexion is necessary in itself and cannot be disjoined—on the contrary, it is in God's power to create satiety without eating, and death without decapitation, and to let life persist notwithstanding the decapitation, and so on with respect to all connexions. The philosophers, however, deny this possibility and claim that that is impossible. To investigate all these innumerable connexions would take us too long, and so we shall choose one single example, namely the burning of cotton through contact with fire; for we regard it as possible that the contact might occur without the burning taking place, and also that the cotton might be changed into ashes without any contact with fire, although the philosophers deny this possibility. The discussion of this matter has three points.

The first is that our opponent claims that the agent of the burning is the fire exclusively; this is a natural, not a voluntary agent, and cannot abstain from what is in its nature when it is brought into contact with a receptive substratum. This we deny, saying: The agent of the burning is God, through His creating the black in the cotton and the disconnexion of its parts, and it is God who made the cotton burn and made it ashes either through the intermediation of angels or without intermediation. For fire is a dead body which has no action, and what is the proof that it is the agent? Indeed, the philosophers have no other proof than the observation of the occurrence of the burning, when there is contact with fire, but observation proves only a simultaneity, not a causation, and, in reality, there is no other cause but God. For there is unanimity of opinion about the fact that the union of the spirit with the perceptive and moving faculties in the sperm of animals does not originate in the natures contained in warmth, cold, moistness, and dryness, and that the father is neither the agent of the embryo through introducing the sperm into the uterus, nor the agent of its life, its sight and hearing, and all its other faculties. And although it is well known that the same faculties exist in the father, still nobody thinks that these faculties exist through him; no, their existence is produced by the First either directly or through the intermediation of the angels who are in charge of these events. Of this fact the philosophers who believe in a creator are quite convinced, but it is precisely with them that we are in dispute.

It has been shown that coexistence does not indicate causation. We shall make this still more clear through an example. Suppose that a man blind from birth, whose eyes are veiled by a membrane and who has never heard people talk of the difference between night and day, has the membrane removed from his eyes by day and sees visible things, he will surely think then that the actual perception in his eyes of the forms of visible things is caused by the opening of his eyelids, and that as long as his sight is sound and in function, the hindrance removed and the object in front of him visible, he will, without doubt, be able to see, and he will never think that he will not see, till, at the moment when the sun sets and the air darkens, he will understand that it was the light of the sun which impressed the visible forms on his sight. And for what other reason do our opponents believe that in the principles of existences there are causes and influences from which the events which coincide with them proceed, than that they are constant, do not disappear, and are not mov-ing bodies which vanish from sight? For if they disappeared or vanished we should observe the disjunction and understand then that behind our percep-tions there exists a cause. And out of this there is no issue, according to the very conclusions of the philosophers themselves.

The true philosophers were therefore unanimously of the opinion that these accidents and events which occur when there is a contact of bodies, or in general a change in their positions, proceed from the bestower of forms who is an angel or a plurality of angels, so that they even said that the impression of the visible forms on the eye occurs through the bestower of forms, and that the rising of the sun, the soundness of the pupil, and the existence of the visible object are only the preparations and dispositions which enable the substratum to receive the forms; and this theory they applied to all events. And this refutes the claim of those who profess that fire is the agent of burning, bread the agent of satiety, medicine the agent of health, and so on.

I say:

To deny the existence of efficient causes which are observed in sensible things is sophistry, and he who defends this doctrine either denies with his tongue what is present in his mind or is carried away by a sophistical doubt which occurs to him concerning this question. For he who denies this can no longer acknowledge that every act must have an agent. The question whether these causes by themselves are sufficient to perform the acts which proceed from them, or need an external cause for the perfection of their act, whether separate or not, is not self-evident and requires much investigation and research. And if the theologians had doubts about the efficient causes which are perceived to cause each other, because there are also effects whose cause is not perceived, this is illogical. Those things whose causes are not perceived are still unknown and must be investigated, precisely because their causes are not perceived; and since everything whose causes are not perceived is still unknown by nature and must be investigated, it follows necessarily that what is not unknown has causes which are perceived. The man who reasons like the theologians does not distinguish between what is self-evident and what is unknown, and everything Ghazali says in this passage is sophistical.

And further, what do the theologians say about the essential causes, the understanding of which alone can make a thing understood? For it is self-evident that things have essences and attributes which determine the special functions of each thing and through which the essences and names of things are differentiated. If a thing had not its specific nature, it would not have a special name nor a definition, and all things would be one—indeed, not even one; for it might be asked whether this one has one special act or one special passivity or not, and if it had a special act, then there would indeed exist special acts proceeding from special natures, but if it had no single special act, then the one would not be one. But if the nature of oneness is denied, the nature of being is denied, and the consequence of the denial of being is nothingness.

Further, are the acts which proceed from all things absolutely necessary for those in whose nature it lies to perform them, or are they only performed in most cases or in half the cases? This is a question which must be investigated, since one single action and passivity between two existent things occurs only through one relation out of an infinite number, and it happens often that one relation hinders another. Therefore it is not absolutely certain that fire acts when it is brought near a sensitive body, for surely it is not improbable that there should be something which stands in such a relation to the sensitive thing as to hinder the action of the fire, as is asserted of talc and other things. But one need not therefore deny fire its burning power so long as fire keeps its name and definition.

Further, it is self-evident that all events have four causes, agent, form, matter, and end, and that they are necessary for the existence of the effects—especially those causes which form a part of the effect, namely that which is called by the philosophers matter, by the theologians condition and substratum, and that which is called by the philosophers form, by the theologians psychological quality. The theologians acknowledge that there exist conditions which are necessary to the conditioned, as when they say that life is a condition of knowledge; and they equally recognize that things have realities and definitions, and that these are necessary for the existence of the existent, and therefore they here judge the visible and the invisible according to one and the same scheme. And they adopt the same attitude towards the consequences of a thing's essence, namely what they call "sign," as for instance when they say that the harmony in the world indicates that its agent possesses mind and that the existence of a world having a design indicates that its agent knows this world. Now intelligence is nothing but the perception of things with their causes, and in this it distinguishes itself from all the other faculties of apprehension, and he who denies causes must deny the intellect. Logic implies the existence of causes and effects, and knowledge of these effects can only be rendered perfect through knowledge of their causes. Denial of cause implies the denial of knowledge, and denial of knowledge implies that nothing in this world can be really known, and that what is supposed to be known is nothing but opinion, that neither proof nor definition exist, and that the essential attributes which compose definitions are void. The man who denies the necessity of any item of knowledge must admit that even this, his own affirmation, is not necessary knowledge.

As to those who admit that there exists, besides necessary knowledge, knowledge which is not necessary, about which the soul forms a judgement on slight evidence and imagines it to be necessary, whereas it is not necessary, the philosophers do not deny this. And if they call such a fact "habit" this may be granted, but otherwise I do not know what they understand by the term "habit"—whether they mean that it is the habit of the agent, the habit of the existing things, or our habit to form a judgement about such things. It is, however, impossible that God should have a habit, for a habit is a custom which the agent acquires and from which a frequent repetition of his act follows, whereas God says in the Holy Book: "Thou shalt not find any alteration in the course of God, and they shall not find any change in the course of God." If they mean a habit in existing things, habit can only exist in the animated; if it exists in something else, it is really a nature, and it is not possible that a thing should have a nature which determined it either necessarily or in most cases. If they mean our habit of forming judgements about things, such a habit is nothing but an act of the soul which is determined by its nature and through which the intellect becomes intellect. The philosophers do not deny such a habit; but "habit" is an ambiguous term, and if it is analysed it means only a hypothetical act; as when we say "So-and-so has the habit of acting in such-and-such a way," meaning that he will act in that way most of the time. If this were true, everything would be the case only by supposition, and there would be no wisdom in the world from which it might be inferred that its agent was wise.

And, as we said, we need not doubt that some of these existents cause each other and act through each other, and that in themselves they do not suffice for their act, but that they are in need of an external agent whose act is a condition of their act, and not only of their act but even of their existence. However, about the essence of this agent or of these agents the philosophers differ in one way, although in another they agree. They all agree in this, that the First Agent is immaterial and that its act is the condition of the existence and acts of existents, and that the act of their agent reaches these existents through the intermediation of an effect of this agent, which is different from these existents and which, according to some of them, is exclusively the heavenly sphere, whereas others assume besides this sphere another immaterial existent which they call the bestower of forms.

But this is not the place to investigate these theories, and the highest part of their inquiry is this; and if you are one of those who desire these truths, then follow the right road which leads to them. The reason why the philosophers differed about the origin of the essential forms and especially of the forms of the soul is that they could not relate them to the warm, cold, moist, and dry, which are the causes of all natural things which come into being and pass away, whereas the materialists related everything which does not seem to have an apparent cause to the warm, cold, moist, and dry, affirming that these things originated through certain mixtures of those elements, just as colours and other accidents come into existence. And the philosophers tried to refute them.[2]

Notes

1. W. M. Watt, trans., *The Faith and Practice of al-Ghazālī* (Oxford: Oneworld, 1994), 29–39.

2. Simon van den Bergh, trans., *Averroes' Tahafut al-Tahafut (The Incoherence of the Incoherence)* (London: Luzac and Co., for the Trustees of the E. J. W. Gibb Memorial, 1954), 316–21.

Commentary

The Importance of al-Ghazālī and Ibn Rushd in the History of Islamic Discourse on Religion and Science

OSMAN BAKAR

Introduction

THE TWO CLASSICAL ISLAMIC TEXTS on which this essay comments are important for our efforts to understand Muslim perspectives on and approaches to the issue of religion and science before the modern era. The texts are from English renderings of two Arabic works written by well-known Muslim thinkers who lived within the same century and during one of the most intellectually active periods in the history of Islam: the Persian al-Ghazālī (1058–1111 CE), and the Andalusian Ibn Rushd (1126–1198 CE), known to the Medieval Latin world as Algazel and Averroes, respectively.[1] The texts are excerpts from al-Ghazālī's *al-Munqidh min al-ḍalāl* (*Deliverance from Error*) and Ibn Rushd's *Tahāfut al-tahāfut* (*The Incoherence of the Incoherence*).[2]

Both Arabic titles are well known in the history of Islamic thought, no doubt partly due to the eminence of their respective authors. Both works are generally viewed by modern scholars of classical Islamic thought as important sources of information about how Muslim minds of the eleventh and the twelfth centuries engaged with issues of scientific knowledge of their day in relation to both religion and philosophy and how they debated with each other on these issues. The main aim of this essay is to discuss the key issues brought up by al-Ghazālī and Ibn Rushd in the two texts and to specifically identify their respective perspectives on and approaches to the issue of the relationship between religion and science.

The Thought of al-Ghazālī and Ibn Rushd:
The Historical–Intellectual Context

Situating the two texts in their historical context will help us better appreciate their significance for the relationship between religion and science during the times of al-Ghazālī and Ibn Rushd as well as during our present time. By the time of al-Ghazālī's birth, four centuries of Islamic history had passed. Scientific activities had flourished to the point of becoming a major feature of the new world civilization that Islam had founded.[3] By slightly over a century after the death of the Prophet Muḥammad (632 CE), science had taken root in the lands of Islam. In the eighth century, state-sponsored scientific activity had begun to take shape, and this was carried out and justified in the name of Islam itself.

Within a relatively short span of time Muslim scientists had made innovations in their respective fields of specialization and expertise. They had added new branches of natural science and mathematics through their creation as independent sciences or academic disciplines, including algebra, trigonometry, optics, mechanics, and civil engineering. The inclusion of these new disciplines in the growing body of scientific knowledge was formalized through the various classifications of knowledge and of the sciences that Muslim scholars produced at various times prior to and after al-Ghazālī.[4] One of these classifications of the sciences was composed by al-Ghazālī himself.[5] In fact, al-Ghazālī's text under discussion here contains his classification of the philosophical sciences into six branches in almost the same manner in which they had been classified by al-Fārābī and Ibn Sīnā, his two most well-known predecessors in philosophy, whom he severely criticized.[6]

Muslim scientists had also broadened the domain of applied science. The most extensive development and progress in the applied sciences occurred in agriculture; practical astronomy; the engineering sciences, which Muslim philosopher-scientists treated as parts of mathematics; and applied or practical medicine. There was extensive application of botany and zoology to agriculture, of mathematics to astronomy and engineering, and of medical science to pharmacology, just to mention the most important examples. By the time of al-Ghazālī, a distinctive scientific culture shaped and colored by Islamic epistemological and moral-ethical values had been well established.

The newly created scientific and research institutions, notably the astronomical observatories and the teaching hospitals, were producing new knowledge as well as systematizing and synthesizing existing knowledge. Intellectual and scientific debates and exchanges of critiques between the different scientists and between the different philosophical-theological schools had become a normal feature of Muslim intellectual life. This aspect of Muslim intellectual life was particularly visible during the century immediately preceding al-Ghazālī's appearance (i.e., 950–1050 CE). This was the age of some of the greatest names in Islamic science and philosophy, including Ibn Sīnā (987 CE–1037 CE), al-Bīrūnī (d. 1051 CE), and the Ikhwān al-Safā' ("Brothers of Purity").[7] The critical scientific debate between Ibn Sīnā and al-Bīrūnī, regarded by leading historians of Islamic science as the two greatest scientific minds in Islam, has been hailed by many as perhaps the most noteworthy of such debates in the history of Islam.

The intellectual dynamism of the period developed largely because scholars and thinkers outside the "scientific community" showed an interest in the scientific issues of the day, thinking of them as having nonscientific implications, particularly religious implications. Al-Ghazālī himself is an excellent example of this point. He was not technically a natural philosopher, as a scientist of his time was generally known. His own expertise was as a jurist and a theologian (*mutakallim*: scholar of the science of *kalām*). His interest in the scientific issues of the day was primarily motivated by philosophical-theological considerations as seen from the perspectives of *kalām*. He was deeply concerned about the philosophical and theological implications of scientific theories for the science of *kalām*, of which he was an eminent representative.

However, the contribution of men of science to the dynamism of the culture of intellectual debate should also be noted. Scientists such as Ibn Sīnā and the Ikhwān al-Safā' were interested in philosophy and theology, but their perspectives were not the same as those of the school of *kalām*. Al-Fārābī (870 CE–950 CE) and Ibn Sīnā belonged to the Peripatetic school of the philosopher-scientists (*al-mashshā'iyyūn*) who were generally considered as the Muslim intellectual followers of Aristotle, although on many issues they differed from his views and interpretations. Al-Ghazālī was a critical thinker. He was critical not only of Muslim Peripatetic philosophy as expounded by al-Fārābī and Ibn Sīnā but also of the Pythagorean school as interpreted by the Ikhwān al-Safā'.

Moreover, he was even critical of some of the views held by many religious scholars in his own Ash'arite school of *kalām*. But he reserved his most severe criticism for the Peripatetics, especially al-Fārābī and Ibn Sīnā, whom he mentions by name in the part of *al-Munqidh* under consideration here.[8]

The prevailing intellectual climate was closely interconnected with the spiritual climate. There was not just an intra-Islamic epistemological pluralism but also a diversity of views regarding posthumous salvation. Al-Ghazālī wrote *al-Munqidh* in such an intellectual and religious climate. Composed a few years before his death, this intellectual autobiography provides an account of his personal and scholarly responses in the course of his life to the diverse intellectual and spiritual phenomena and challenges in the Islamic world of his time in general and in his native Persia in particular.[9] The central theme of *al-Munqidh* was his first personal crisis, which was epistemological in nature, and his second personal crisis, which was spiritual in nature.[10]

The epistemological crisis led him to study the epistemologies of all the major intellectual schools of his time, including Muslim Peripatetic epistemology. His spiritual crisis led to his full conversion to Sufism, embarking on the Sufi path to salvation and leading an ascetic and contemplative life. The limited concern of this essay allows us to deal only with an aspect of the epistemological crisis. This aspect pertains to his critique of the philosophical sciences, which cover much of what we understand today as science. This critique constitutes the core of our selected text from *al-Munqidh*. It is in this text that we find a brief reference to a philosophical-scientific issue that lies at the heart of the epistemological conflict between the school of *kalām* and the school of *falsafa* (Peripatetic philosophy). The issue in question is the idea of causality, which necessarily brings up the issue of the divine cause and the natural causes in the cause–effect chains observable in the world of nature.

Al-Ghazālī does not explicitly mention in this text the issue of causality, but he is obviously referring to it when, in his brief discussion of natural science, he explains that his objections to the Peripatetic philosopher-scientists on a number of issues were based on "the recognition that nature is in subjection to God most high, not acting of itself but serving as an instrument in the hands of its Creator."[11] This is just a passing remark, but in the same context al-Ghazālī points out that he has provided a detailed discussion of the issue in his critique of the Peripatetic philosophy of science titled "The Incoherence of the Philosophers" (*Tahāfut al-falāsifa*).

Less than a century after al-Ghazālī's death, Ibn Rushd wrote "The Incoherence of the Incoherence" (*Tahāfut al-tahāfut*) with the intention of refuting
many of the views presented by al-Ghazālī in *Tahāfut al-falāsifa*. The text from
Tahāfut al-tahāfut under consideration here clearly explains the Peripatetic
position on causality. Ibn Rushd, who is considered the most loyal Muslim
follower of Aristotle, philosophically and scientifically speaking, clearly reflects
the Aristotelian understanding of causality in his own treatment of this
subject.

Al-Ghazālī and Ibn Rushd on Causality

Causality was very important to Peripatetic science. The Peripatetic philosopher-
scientists tried to explain all natural phenomena in terms of the cause–effect
principle, according to which the existence of a natural thing or the occurrence
of a natural event or phenomenon is due to four causes: material, formal,
efficient, and final. The efficient cause refers to the agent of the act that results
in the effect. Regarding this principle, Ibn Rushd writes in our selected text
from *Tahāfut al-tahāfut*: "It is self-evident that all events have four causes,
agent, form, matter, and end, and that they are necessary for the existence of
the effects—especially those causes which form a part of the effect, namely
that which is called by the philosophers matter, by the theologians condition
and substratum, and that which is called by the philosophers form, by the
theologians psychological quality."[12]

To illustrate the four causes, let us take the simple example of the existence
of a wooden table. The material cause of the table would be wood, the material
of which the table is made. The formal cause would be the shape of the table.
Its efficient cause would be the carpenter who crafts the wood into a thing
with the shape of a table. The final cause would be the purpose of the table.
This example is easily understood to explain the principle of causality since it
is taken from the world of physical objects created by man. But when the
object under consideration is not man-made but natural, and when all the
causes are natural, then the identities of the four causes in question and their
relations would be more difficult to comprehend. This, however, is the chief
concern of Peripatetic science.

The main task of science, as seen by the Peripatetic scientists, is to identify
the four causes and their properties. In their view no science would be possible

if we were to dispense with the principle of causality in the sense just defined. For this reason, they strongly opposed any other perspective on the study of the natural world that did not find any necessity in their principle of causality. This explains the passion with which, in *Tahāfut al-tahāfut*, Ibn Rushd seeks to refute al-Ghazālī's arguments against causality in *Tahāfut al-falāsifa*.

Central to the Peripatetic idea of causality is the notion of the efficient cause. Thus in his reply to al-Ghazālī, Ibn Rushd concentrates on the defense of the efficient cause and the refutation of the former's denial of this type of cause. Al-Ghazālī's denial of causality rests on the following arguments: in his own words, (1) "the connection between what is usually believed to be a cause and what is believed to be an effect is not a necessary connection; each of the two things [i.e., cause and effect] has its own individuality and is not the other";[13] (2) "coexistence does not indicate causation";[14] (3) the necessary connection is the divine will and the divine power "for the connection in these things is based on a prior power of God to create them in a successive order, though not because this connection is necessary in itself and cannot be disjoined";[15] (4) in the natural world things exist and events occur because they proceed from "the First either directly or through the intermediation of the angels who are in charge of these events";[16] and (5) the angels are "the bestower of forms."[17]

What al-Ghazālī seeks to emphasize in these passages is that God alone is the agent or the efficient cause. Even when he concedes the intermediary role of the angels in the natural world, he would like others to acknowledge the fact that in reality it is God who is the efficient cause since he created the angels as his intermediary agents. In defense of this central argument in his denial of causality, al-Ghazālī emphasizes that what appears to man as a cause-and-effect relationship is nothing more than the habit of his mind to see the thing called cause and the thing called effect as indeed having such a relationship. Quite obviously, theology is the main consideration in al-Ghazālī's denial of causality. By implication, he wants science to be theocentric. Further support for this view can be found in the rest of *Tahāfut al-falāsifa*, where al-Ghazālī is concerned with the weakening and the corruption of the Muslim faith, which he attributes to the faulty Muslim view of science and of its relationship with religion, among other causes.

In the selected text from *al-Munqidh* al-Ghazālī addresses some of these faulty views particularly in his discussion of mathematics, natural science, and metaphysics. He appears to favor a scientific picture of the natural world based on another kind of causality in which the role of the secondary agents or efficient cause is marginal and the divine role is central, thus categorically rejecting the Peripatetic notion of efficient cause in favor of the idea of God as the dominant efficient cause. Critics of al-Ghazālī's position question the feasibility of such a science, but its proponents and sympathizers argue that the schools of *kalām* have produced numerous writings on atomistic cosmology and atomistic physics that, interestingly enough, share many features with contemporary quantum physics.

In his response to al-Ghazālī's denial of causality, Ibn Rushd stresses the following points: (1) "Logic implies the existence of causes and effects, and knowledge of these effects can only be rendered perfect through knowledge of their causes. Denial of cause implies the denial of knowledge, and denial of knowledge implies that nothing in this world can really be known, and that what is supposed to be known is nothing but opinion, that neither proof nor definition exist, and that the essential attributes which compose definitions are void";[18] (2) "To deny the existence of efficient causes which are observed in sensible things is sophistry, and he who defends this doctrine either denies with his tongue what is present in his mind or is carried away by a sophistical doubt which occurs to him concerning this question. For he who denies this can no longer acknowledge that every act must have an agent";[19] (3) "It is self-evident that things have essences and attributes which determine the special functions of each thing and through which the essences and names of things are differentiated. If a thing had not its specific nature, it would not have a special name nor a definition, and all things would be one—indeed, not even one";[20] and (4) the philosophers all agree that "the First Agent is immaterial and that its act is the condition of the existence and acts of existents, and that the act of their agent reaches these existents through the intermediation of an effect of this agent, which is different from these existents and which, according to some of them, is exclusively the heavenly sphere, whereas others assume besides this sphere another immaterial existent which they call the bestower of forms."[21]

Conclusion

We may infer from the salient arguments presented by al-Ghazālī and Ibn Rushd that their main dispute concerning causality is about the nature and reality of the central agent or efficient cause that is to play the dominant role in their respective sciences, whether it should be God as the First Agent and the immaterial and invisible intermediary agents or the natural secondary agents. But they also share significant views. They agree that God is the First Agent and that there are immaterial intermediary agents that they identify with the "bestower of forms," although they differ on the precise identities of these intermediary agents. For both of them, science is ultimately based upon the divine reality.

Through his detailed studies of *kalām* and *falsafa* al-Ghazālī was persuaded to formulate a new epistemology for each of these sciences and to redraw the boundaries of science in conformity with the new epistemology. The new epistemology that he in fact did formulate, but which is beyond the scope of this essay, sought to reaffirm the subordination of reason to divine revelation, a doctrine that in his view had been undermined by the Muslim Peripatetic philosopher-scientists.

For Further Reflection

1. What are the main features of the theological orthodoxy that al-Ghazālī seeks to defend?
2. What are the main points in al-Ghazālī's critique of the philosophers?
3. What can we infer about al-Ghazālī's philosophy of science from the text?
4. Does al-Ghazālī provide an accurate account of both Greek philosophy and the Muslim philosophies of science current in his time?
5. How critical is Aristotelian causality to science?
6. What is the significance for contemporary Muslim thought of the differences between al-Ghazālī and Ibn Rushd illustrated by these texts?

Notes

1. For a detailed account of the life, works, and significance of al-Ghazālī, see Osman Bakar, *Classification of Knowledge in Islam* (Cambridge: Islamic Texts Society, 1998), ch. 7. For the life, works, and significance of Ibn Rushd, see Majid Fakhry, *Averroes (Ibn Rushd): His Life, Works and Influence* (Oxford: Oneworld Publications, 2001).

2. See W. M. Watt, trans., *The Faith and Practice of al-Ghazālī* (London: Allen & Unwin, 1953). This translation has seen numerous reprints since its first publication. The first English

translation of *al-Munqidh min al-ḍalāl* was made available by Claud Field. See Claud Field, trans., *The Confessions of al-Ghazali* (London: John Murray, 1909). Another translation, which is richly annotated, is by Richard Joseph McCarthy. See R. J. McCarthy, trans., *Freedom and Fulfillment: An Annotated Translation of al-Munqidh min al-Dalal and Other Relevant Works of al-Ghazali* (Boston: Twayne Publishers, 1980). Citations here refer to W. Montgomery Watt, *Al-Ghazālī: Deliverance from Error and the Beginning of Guidance* (Kuala Lumpur: Islamic Book Trust, 2005), 16–27. For the Ibn Rushd text, see Simon van den Bergh, trans., *Averroes' Tahafut al-Tahafut (The Incoherence of the Incoherence)* (London: Luzac and Co., for the Trustees of the E. J. W. Gibb Memorial, 1954).

3. For a good introductory account of the historical development and important features of scientific activities in the first four centuries of Islam, especially in their relations to the spiritual and societal teachings of Islam, see Seyyed Hossein Nasr, *Islamic Science: An Illustrated Study* (London: World of Islam Festival Publishing Co., Thorsons Publisher Ltd., 1976).

4. For a comprehensive study of the Muslim classifications of the sciences in classical Islam, see Bakar, *Classification of Knowledge in Islam*.

5. For a detailed study of al-Ghazālī's classification of knowledge (*'ilm*) and of the sciences (*'ulūm*), see Bakar, *Classification of Knowledge*, ch. 8 and 9.

6. Watt, *Al-Ghazālī*, 20–27.

7. For a detailed comparative study of these philosophers and scientists, see Seyyed Hossein Nasr, *An Introduction to Islamic Cosmological Doctrines* (Cambridge: Harvard University Press, 1964).

8. Watt, *Al-Ghazālī*, 20.

9. Al-Ghazālī wrote *al-Munqidh* in Naishapur between 1106 CE and 1110 CE after his return to public teaching at the Nizamiyyah Madrasa there following a decade-long period of spiritual retreat.

10. For a detailed study of the nature and significance of these two personal crises of al-Ghazālī, see Osman Bakar, *Tawhid and Science: Islamic Perspectives on Religion and Science* (Shah Alam: ARAH Publications, 2008), 2nd ed., ch. 3.

11. Watt, *Al-Ghazālī*, 25.

12. Van den Bergh, *Averroes' Tahafut al-Tahafut*, 319.

13. Ibid., 316.

14. Ibid., 317.

15. Ibid., 316.

16. Ibid., 316.

17. Ibid., 320.

18. Ibid., 318.

19. Ibid., 317.

20. Ibid., 317.

21. Ibid., 320.

Charles Darwin

From *The Descent of Man*, Chapter 3

Belief in God—Religion

THERE IS NO EVIDENCE that man was aboriginally endowed with the ennobling belief in the existence of an Omnipotent God. On the contrary there is ample evidence, derived not from hasty travellers, but from men who have long resided with savages, that numerous races have existed, and still exist, who have no idea of one or more gods, and who have no words in their languages to express such an idea. The question is of course wholly distinct from that higher one, whether there exists a Creator and Ruler of the universe; and this has been answered in the affirmative by some of the highest intellects that have ever existed.

If, however, we include under the term "religion" the belief in unseen or spiritual agencies the case is wholly different; for this belief seems to be universal with the less civilised races. Nor is it difficult to comprehend how it arose. As soon as the important faculties of the imagination, wonder, and curiosity, together with some power of reasoning, had become partially developed, man would naturally crave to understand what was passing around him, and would have vaguely speculated on his own existence. As Mr. M'Lennan has remarked, "Some explanation of the phenomena of life, a man must feign for himself, and to judge from the universality of it, the simplest hypothesis, and the first to occur to men, seems to have been that natural phenomena are ascribable to the presence in animals, plants, and things, and in the forces of nature, of such spirits prompting to action as men are conscious they themselves possess." It is also probable, as Mr. Tylor has shewn, that dreams may have first given rise to the notion of spirits; for savages do not readily distinguish between subjective and objective impressions. When a savage dreams, the figures which appear before him are believed to have come from a distance, and to stand over him; or "the soul of the dreamer goes out on its travels, and

111

comes home with a remembrance of what it has seen." But until the faculties of imagination, curiosity, reason, &c., had been fairly well developed in the mind of man, his dreams would not have led him to believe in spirits, any more than in the case of a dog.

The tendency in savages to imagine that natural objects and agencies are animated by spiritual or living essences is perhaps illustrated by a little fact which I once noticed: my dog, a full-grown and very sensible animal, was lying on the lawn during a hot and still day; but at a little distance a slight breeze occasionally moved an open parasol, which would have been wholly disregarded by the dog, had any one stood near it. As it was, every time that the parasol slightly moved, the dog growled fiercely and barked. He must, I think, have reasoned to himself in a rapid and unconscious manner, that movement without any apparent cause indicated the presence of some strange living agent, and that no stranger had a right to be on his territory.

The belief in spiritual agencies would easily pass into the belief in the existence of one or more gods. For savages would naturally attribute to spirits the same passions, the same love of vengeance or simplest form of justice, and the same affections which they themselves feel. The Fuegians appear to be in this respect in an intermediate condition, for when the surgeon on board the Beagle shot some young ducklings as specimens, York Minster declared in the most solemn manner, "Oh, Mr. Bynoe, much rain, much snow, blow much"; and this was evidently a retributive punishment for wasting human food. So again he related how, when his brother killed a "wild man," storms long raged, much rain and snow fell. Yet we could never discover that the Fuegians believed in what we should call a God, or practised any religious rites; and Jemmy Button, with justifiable pride, stoutly maintained that there was no devil in his land. This latter assertion is the more remarkable, as with savages the belief in bad spirits is far more common than that in good ones.

The feeling of religious devotion is a highly complex one, consisting of love, complete submission to an exalted and mysterious superior, a strong sense of dependence, fear, reverence, gratitude, hope for the future, and perhaps other elements. No being could experience so complex an emotion until advanced in his intellectual and moral faculties to at least a moderately high level. Nevertheless, we see some distant approach to this state of mind in the deep love of a dog for his master, associated with complete submission, some fear, and perhaps other feelings. The behaviour of a dog when returning to his master after an absence, and, as I may add, of a monkey to his beloved keeper, is widely different from that towards their fellows. In the latter case the transports of joy appear to be somewhat less, and the sense of equality is shewn in every action. Professor Braubach goes so far as to maintain that a dog looks on his master as on a god.

The same high mental faculties which first led man to believe in unseen spiritual agencies, then in fetishism, polytheism, and ultimately in monotheism, would infallibly lead him, as long as his reasoning powers remained poorly developed, to various strange superstitions and customs. Many of these are terrible to think of—such as the sacrifice of human beings to a blood-loving god; the trial of innocent persons by the ordeal of poison or fire; witchcraft, &c.—yet it is well occasionally to reflect on these superstitions, for they shew us what an infinite debt of gratitude we owe to the improvement of our reason, to science, and to our accumulated knowledge. As Sir J. Lubbock has well observed, "it is not too much to say that the horrible dread of unknown evil hangs like a thick cloud over savage life, and embitters every pleasure." These miserable and indirect consequences of our highest faculties may be compared with the incidental and occasional mistakes of the instincts of the lower animals.[1]

Two Letters

Letter from Charles Darwin to Asa Gray (May 22, 1860)

. . . With respect to the theological view of the question; this is always painful to me.—I am bewildered.—I had no intention to write atheistically. But I own that I cannot see, as plainly as others do, & as I shd wish to do, evidence of design & beneficence on all sides of us. There seems to me too much misery in the world. I cannot persuade myself that a beneficent & omnipotent God would have designedly created the Ichneumonidæ with the express intention of their feeding within the living bodies of caterpillars, or that a cat should play with mice. Not believing this, I see no necessity in the belief that the eye was expressly designed. On the other hand I cannot anyhow be contented to view this wonderful universe & especially the nature of man, & to conclude that everything is the result of brute force. I am inclined to look at everything as resulting from designed laws, with the details, whether good or bad, left to the working out of what we may call chance. Not that this notion *at all* satisfies me. I feel most deeply that the whole subject is too profound for the human intellect. A dog might as well speculate on the mind of Newton.—Let each man hope & believe what he can.—

Certainly I agree with you that my views are not at all necessarily atheistical. The lightning kills a man, whether a good one or bad one, owing to the excessively complex action of natural laws,—a child (who may turn out an idiot) is born by action of even more complex laws,—and I can see no reason, why a man, or other animal, may not have been aboriginally produced by other laws; & that all these laws may have been expressly designed by an omniscient Creator, who foresaw every future event & consequence. But the more I think the more bewildered I become; as indeed I have probably shown by this letter.[2]

Letter from Charles Darwin to John Fordyce (May 7, 1879)

It seems to me absurd to doubt that a man may be an ardent Theist & an evolutionist.—You are right about Kingsley. Asa Gray, the eminent botanist, is another case in point—What my own views may be is a question of no consequence to any one except myself.—But as you ask, I may state that my judgment often fluctuates. Moreover whether a man deserves to be called a theist depends on the definition of the term: which is much too large a subject for a note. In my most extreme fluctuations I have never been an atheist in the sense of denying the existence of a God.—I think that generally (& more and more so as I grow older) but not always, that an agnostic would be the most correct description of my state of mind.[3]

From Charles Darwin's Autobiography

Religious Belief

During these two years [October 1836–January 1839] I was led to think much about religion. Whilst on board the *Beagle* I was quite orthodox, and I remember being heartily laughed at by several of the officers (though themselves orthodox) for quoting the Bible as an unanswerable authority on some point of morality. I suppose it was the novelty of the argument that amused them. But I had gradually come, by this time, to see that the Old Testament from its manifestly false history of the world, with the Tower of Babel, the rainbow as a sign, etc., etc., and from its attributing to God the feelings of a revengeful tyrant, was no more to be trusted than the sacred books of the Hindoos, or the beliefs of any barbarian. The question then continually rose before my mind and would not be banished,—is it credible that if God were now to make a revelation to the Hindoos, would he permit it to be connected with the belief in Vishnu, Siva, &c., as Christianity is connected with the Old Testament. This appeared to me utterly incredible.

By further reflecting that the clearest evidence would be requisite to make any sane man believe in the miracles by which Christianity is supported,—that the more we know of the fixed laws of nature the more incredible do miracles become,—that the men at that time were ignorant and credulous to a degree almost incomprehensible by us,—that the Gospels cannot be proved to have been written simultaneously with the events,—that they differ in many important details, far too important as it seemed to me to be admitted as the usual inaccuracies of eye-witnesses;—by such reflections as these, which I give not as having the least novelty or value, but as they influenced me, I gradually came to disbelieve in Christianity as a divine revelation. The fact that many false religions have spread over large portions of the earth like wild-fire had some weight with me. Beautiful as is the morality of the New Testament, it can hardly be denied that its perfection depends in part on the interpretation which we now put on metaphors and allegories.

But I was very unwilling to give up my belief;—I feel sure of this for I can well remember often and often inventing day-dreams of old letters between distinguished Romans and manuscripts being discovered at Pompeii or elsewhere which confirmed in the most striking manner all that was written in the Gospels. But I found it more and more difficult, with free scope given to my imagination, to invent evidence which would suffice to convince me. Thus disbelief crept over me at a very slow rate, but was at last complete. The rate was so slow that I felt no distress, and have never since doubted even for a single second that my conclusion was correct. I can indeed hardly see how anyone ought to wish Christianity to be true; for if so the plain language of the text seems to show that the men who do not believe, and this would include my Father, Brother and almost all my best friends, will be everlastingly punished.

And this is a damnable doctrine.

Although I did not think much about the existence of a personal God until a considerably later period of my life, I will here give the vague conclusions to which I have been driven. The old argument of design in nature, as given by Paley, which formerly seemed to me so conclusive, fails, now that the law of natural selection has been discovered. We can no longer argue that, for instance, the beautiful hinge of a bivalve shell must have been made by an intelligent being, like the hinge of a door by man. There seems to be no more design in the variability of organic beings and in the action of natural selection, than in the course which the wind blows. Everything in nature is the result of fixed laws.

But I have discussed this subject at the end of my book on the *Variation of Domestic Animals and Plants*, and the argument there given has never, as far as I can see, been answered.

But passing over the endless beautiful adaptations which we everywhere meet with, it may be asked how can the generally beneficent arrangement of the world be accounted for? Some writers indeed are so much impressed with the amount of suffering in the world, that they doubt if we look to all sentient beings, whether there is more of misery or of happiness;—whether the world as a whole is a good or a bad one. According to my judgment happiness decidedly prevails, though this would be very difficult to prove. If the truth of this conclusion be granted, it harmonises well with the effects which we might expect from natural selection. If all the individuals of any species were habitually to suffer to an extreme degree they would neglect to propagate their kind; but we have no reason to believe that this has ever or at least often occurred. Some other considerations, moreover, lead to the belief that all sentient beings have been formed so as to enjoy, as a general rule, happiness.

Every one who believes, as I do, that all the corporeal and mental organs (excepting those which are neither advantageous or disadvantageous to the possessor) of all beings have been developed through natural selection, or the survival of the fittest, together with use or habit, will admit that these organs have been formed so that their possessors may compete successfully with other beings, and thus increase in number. Now an animal may be led to pursue that course of action which is the most beneficial to the species by suffering, such as pain, hunger, thirst, and fear,—or by pleasure, as in eating and drinking and in the propagation of the species, &c. or by both means combined, as in the search for food. But pain or suffering of any kind, if long continued, causes depression and lessens the power of action; yet is well adapted to make a creature guard itself against any great or sudden evil. Pleasurable sensations, on the other hand, may be long continued without any depressing effect; on the contrary they stimulate the whole system to increased action. Hence it has come to pass that most or all sentient beings have been developed in such a manner through natural selection, that pleasurable sensations serve as their habitual guides. We see this in the pleasure from exertion, even occasionally from great exertion of the body or mind,—in the pleasure of our daily meals, and especially in the pleasure derived from sociability and from loving our families. The sum of such pleasures as these, which are habitual or frequently recurrent, give, as I can hardly doubt, to most sentient beings an excess of happiness over misery, although many occasionally suffer much. Such suffering, is quite compatible with the belief in Natural Selection, which is not perfect in its action, but tends only to render each species as successful as possible in the battle for life with other species, in wonderfully complex and changing circumstances.

That there is much suffering in the world no one disputes. Some have attempted to explain this in reference to man by imagining that it serves for his moral improvement. But the number of men in the world is as nothing compared with that of all other sentient beings, and these often suffer greatly without any moral improvement. A being so powerful and so full of knowledge as a God who could create the universe, is to our finite minds omnipotent and omniscient, and it revolts our understanding to suppose that his benevolence is not unbounded, for what advantage can there be in the sufferings of millions of the lower animals throughout almost endless time? This very old argument from the existence of suffering against the existence of an intelligent first cause seems to me a strong one; whereas, as just remarked, the presence of much suffering agrees well with the view that all organic beings have been developed through variation and natural selection.

At the present day the most usual argument for the existence of an intelligent God is drawn from the deep inward conviction and feelings which are experienced by most persons. But it cannot be doubted that Hindoos, Mahomadans and others might argue in the same manner and with equal force in favour of the existence of one God, or of many Gods, or as with the Buddists of no God. There are also many barbarian tribes who cannot be said with any truth to believe in what we call God: they believe indeed in spirits or ghosts, and it can be explained, as Tyler and Herbert Spencer have shown, how such a belief would be likely to arise.

Formerly I was led by feelings such as those just referred to (although I do not think that the religious sentiment was ever strongly developed in me), to the firm conviction of the existence of God, and of the immortality of the soul. In my Journal I wrote that whilst standing in the midst of the grandeur of a Brazilian forest, "it is not possible to give an adequate idea of the higher feelings of wonder, admiration, and devotion which fill and elevate the mind." I well remember my conviction that there is more in man than the mere breath of his body. But now the grandest scenes would not cause any such convictions and feelings to rise in my mind. It may be truly said that I am like a man who has become colour-blind, and the universal belief by men of the existence of redness makes my present loss of perception of not the least value as evidence. This argument would be a valid one if all men of all races had the same inward conviction of the existence of one God; but we know that this is very far from being the case. Therefore I cannot see that such inward convictions and feelings are of any weight as evidence of what really exists. The state of mind which grand scenes formerly excited in me, and which was intimately connected with a belief in God, did not essentially differ from that which is often called the sense of sublimity; and however difficult it may be to explain the genesis of this sense, it can hardly be advanced as an argument for the existence of God, any more than the powerful though vague and similar feelings excited by music.

With respect to immortality, nothing shows me how strong and almost instinctive a belief it is, as the consideration of the view now held by most physicists, namely that the sun with all the planets will in time grow too cold for life, unless indeed some great body dashes into the sun and thus gives it fresh life.—Believing as I do that man in the distant future will be a far more perfect creature than he now is, it is an intolerable thought that he and all other sentient beings are doomed to complete annihilation after such long-continued slow progress. To those who fully admit the immortality of the human soul, the destruction of our world will not appear so dreadful.

Another source of conviction in the existence of God, connected with the reason and not with the feelings, impresses me as having much more weight. This follows from the extreme difficulty or rather impossibility of conceiving this immense and wonderful universe, including man with his capacity of looking far backwards and far into futurity, as the result of blind chance or necessity. When thus reflecting I feel compelled to look to a First Cause having an intelligent mind in some degree analogous to that of man; and I deserve to be called a Theist.

This conclusion was strong in my mind about the time, as far as I can remember, when I wrote the *Origin of Species*; and it is since that time that it has very gradually with many fluctuations become weaker. But then arises the doubt—can the mind of man, which has, as I fully believe, been developed from a mind as low as that possessed by the lowest animal, be trusted when it draws such grand conclusions? May not these be the result of the connection between cause and effect which strikes us as a necessary one, but probably depends merely on inherited experience? Nor must we overlook the probability of the constant inculcation in a belief in God on the minds of children producing so strong and perhaps an inherited effect on their brains not yet fully developed, that it would be as difficult for them to throw off their belief in God, as for a monkey to throw off its instinctive fear and hatred of a snake.

I cannot pretend to throw the least light on such abstruse problems. The mystery of the beginning of all things is insoluble by us; and I for one must be content to remain an Agnostic.[4]

Notes

1. Charles Darwin, *The Descent of Man*, "Comparison of the Mental Powers of Man and the Lower Animals," ch. 3. The Online Literature Library, accessed September 8, 2011, www.literature.org/authors/darwin-charles/the-descent-of-man/chapter-03.html.

2. Letter 2814, Darwin Correspondence Project, accessed September 8, 2011, www.darwinproject.ac.uk/entry-2814.

3. Letter 12041, Darwin Correspondence Project, accessed September 8, 2011, www.darwinproject.ac.uk/entry-12041.

4. *The Autobiography of Charles Darwin (1809–1882)* (London: Collins, 1958), 85–94.

Introduction to Darwin and the Selected Texts

JOHN HEDLEY BROOKE

THE WORK OF CHARLES DARWIN impinged on many aspects of Christian culture.[1] Two questions in particular were seen in a new light. Is there a clear line of demarcation between humans and animals, as had often been supposed? And can scientific advances raise issues that may, or should, affect our moral judgment? For many, Darwin's theory of evolution by natural selection, more than any previous scientific innovation, changed perceptions about how these questions should be answered. This was primarily because Darwin's theory of "descent with modification," as he described it, postulated a historical continuum between humans and their animal ancestors. There was a deep challenge to the anthropocentric assumptions that had informed so much of Western culture and Christian natural theology in particular.[2] On the moral question it was clear to Darwin that the problem of animal suffering had to be taken more seriously, especially given the tortuous, bloodstained trail of evolution. Whereas in the human case suffering had sometimes been rationalized by saying it was conducive to moral improvement, this was not an argument that was obviously applicable to animals.[3]

There is a well-known irony in Darwin's biography that he recognized himself. During his time at Cambridge University, which followed an abortive start to a medical career at Edinburgh, Darwin's intention was to become a clergyman in the Church of England.[4] He said of his beliefs at that time that they were "orthodox." His scientific mentors in Cambridge, John Henslow and Adam Sedgwick, subscribed to a view of the world in which the many adaptations and apparent designs in organic systems were the direct result of divine power and wisdom. The irony is that Darwin later had to endure stinging attacks from members of the clergy (including Sedgwick) for his naturalistic account of the origin of species.[5] Darwin himself had gradually given up the idea of becoming a priest during his five-year voyage on HMS *Beagle* when he fully exploited the opportunity to study natural history in depth. It is well known that, in South America in particular, Darwin was struck by the similarities between fossil forms and existing species that resembled them. He was staggered, too, by the sheer amount of extinction that could be discerned from the fossil record. Crucially, he was struck by the fact that the species found on islands most closely resembled those of the nearest mainland, from which Darwin supposed they had migrated, gradually to diversify in their new environments. It would, however, be wrong to conclude that Darwin had a "eureka" moment when he visited the Galapagos archipelago because we now know that he initially muddled his specimens of the famous finches, not having anticipated the insight that it would be possible to tell, just by inspecting a tortoise or bird, from which island it came.[6]

Two elements in Darwin's biography are particularly significant when considering his religious outlook and how it changed over time. During the *Beagle* voyage he witnessed many aspects of what he later called the "struggle for existence." A wretched example was afforded by natives of the Tierra del Fuego, who eked out a meager existence in one of the most inhospitable climates on Earth. Darwin was deeply interested in them because, on board ship, were three Fuegians who had been taken back to England by Captain Robert Fitzroy from an earlier surveying expedition. They had been "civilized," exposed to Christian teaching and values, and were now being returned, in the company of a missionary, to evangelize their own people. As it happened, this evangelical experiment ended in disaster and the missionary had to flee for his life.[7] But the experience was important for Darwin in at least two respects. Arguably, it helped him to appreciate how thin was the veneer of civilization. "Were our ancestors men like these?" he would ask. More importantly, on studying the native Fuegians closely, he concluded that they neither had a word for God nor appeared to take part in any form of religious ritual. This challenged the common view, vouchsafed to Darwin by his cousin, Hensleigh Wedgwood, that humans differ from animals in one decisive respect. Humans had an innate sense of God whereas animals did not. Darwin was no longer so sure; many years later, when he wrote about religion in his *Descent of Man* (1871), he would return to this theme. References to the Fuegians Jemmy Button and York Minster occur in the appended extract from the *Descent*.

The second element in Darwin's biography that deserves special attention has more to do with the moral considerations that weighed with him as he gradually renounced Christianity in favor, first, of a nonbiblical deism and, eventually, agnosticism.[8] It is often supposed that Darwin rejected the Christian faith simply because of his science, but the evidence from the appended texts suggests otherwise. His primary objection was moral. He came to despise the doctrine that heaven was only for the orthodox believer while free thinkers (which would include his grandfather, father, and brother) were destined for eternal damnation. Between 1849 and early 1851 Darwin lost both his father (which focused his mind on this "damnable doctrine") and his cherished daughter, Annie, at the tender age of ten. The consequence was a final renunciation of the faith that was still so dear to his wife, Emma.[9]

This is not to say that Darwin's science was irrelevant to the way he approached religious questions. His scientific mentality meant that he found it difficult to take miracle stories seriously. It is also true that his concept of natural selection eviscerated one of William Paley's arguments for design: the argument from adaptive contrivances in organic systems to a transcendent Contriver. Even so, at the time Darwin wrote his *Origin of Species*, he was still willing to countenance the view that the *laws* of nature were designed by a Creator.[10] In the responses to this, his most famous book, we can see the principal concerns of those who protested in the name of the Christian religion.

For those not yet accustomed to the view that the Bible contains many different literary genres, and not yet accustomed to seeing the Genesis Creation narratives as conveying a profound myth about the human condition, the clash between Darwin's theory and a literal reading of the text was deeply disturbing.[11] There were even highly educated naturalists among Darwin's friends who asked him for advice on how to interpret the story of Eve's derivation from Adam's rib.[12] It was also recognized that if natural selection was the perfecting mechanism Darwin had described, if natural selection could counterfeit design, then a traditional natural theology was embarrassed. Revision was certainly possible, as it was for Charles Kingsley and Frederick Temple, both of whom rejoiced in the fact that God was now so much wiser: "He" could make things *make themselves*.[13] In the background, however, there was the worrying emphasis on seemingly random events in nature, which made it more difficult to believe there had been a blueprint for creation.

A third problem was that indicated at the outset. What would it mean now to speak of human beings made in the image of God? For Samuel Wilberforce, Bishop of Oxford, Darwin's theory was an affront to human dignity and "utterly irreconcilable" with the status accorded humanity by Christ's assumption of human form.[14] Wilberforce made the mistake of assuming that if humans were derived from animals, they could not have evolved to a state of being with higher capacities, but his encounter with T. H. Huxley at the 1860 meeting of the British Association in Oxford has, regrettably, come to epitomize what in reality was a diverse Christian response.[15] F. W. Farrar, who preached the funeral sermon when Darwin was buried in Westminster Abbey, recalled that, even before Darwin's death in 1882, the theory of evolution had been "admitted as a possible explanation of the phenomena of life by leading theologians." Farrar added that "we have been told on all sides that, if it should prove to be true, there is nothing in it which is contrary to the creeds of the Catholic faith."[16] Farrar contrasted the shining example of Darwin's forbearance with the contemptuous denunciation in some clerical reactions. Farrar may even have had Samuel Wilberforce in mind because he had been present at the Oxford debate in 1860.

All who took the Darwinian theory seriously, however, had to recognize that, as a method of creation, evolution as Darwin described it raised difficult questions. Is this how one could reasonably expect an omnipotent God to have proceeded? Darwin's disciple in the study of animal behavior, George Romanes, provides a sensitive illustration of the difficulty. Vacillating between theism and agnosticism, Romanes conceded that the greatest problem Darwin had raised was that the nature of the deity, inferred on the basis of the theory alone, was far removed from that supposed in the noblest forms of religion.[17]

That is, of course, a very brief summary. Different problems affected different commentators in very different ways, according to their own backgrounds, locations, and sensibilities.[18] But let us now turn to the texts. Darwin made very few public statements about religion, but the extract from his *Descent of Man* is one of them. This shows Darwin drawing on the work of anthropologists and underlining the point that had struck him so forcibly about the Fuegians nearly forty years before: their lack of an innate sense of God.

The two letters, to Asa Gray and James Fordyce, show that although Darwin had rejected Christianity, he did not regard himself as an atheist. He also states in the letter to Fordyce that it would be "absurd" to doubt that one can be an ardent theist and an evolutionist. When contrasting naturalism with theism, as many modern commentators do, it becomes important to ask what is meant by "nature." At the time he wrote the *Origin*, the word did not mean for Darwin what it means for most modern Darwinians. In his large book on species, which was never published because writing the *Origin* intervened when Darwin was threatened by the prospect of being scooped by Alfred Russel Wallace, Darwin gave an explicit definition of "nature": "By nature I mean the laws ordained by God to govern the universe."[19] Naturalism and theism did not have to be mutually exclusive.

Darwin wrote his autobiography for members of his family, not for public consumption. The chosen extract gives probably the fullest account we have of his gradual loss of faith and the reasons for it. As indicated earlier, it can be surprising to find what an apparently low profile his science has in those reasons for his rejection of Christianity. There are other points worth highlighting from these texts. From the *Descent of Man* we should note that Darwin does describe belief in an omnipotent God as an "ennobling" belief, not a harmful superstition. There is also the important distinction he makes in the first paragraph of the extract. The question, he says, whether there exists a Creator and Ruler of the universe is a higher question than questions about religious beliefs or lack of them among the savages. It is to be understood that there is a long tradition of affirming a Creator and that some of the best intellects have made that affirmation. Darwin followed David Hume in asserting a trajectory from animism to polytheism to monotheism in the religious development of humanity. That does cut across a simple natural theology in which belief in one God is said to be natural or innate. There is resonance again with Darwin's scepticism about an inherent biological basis for monotheism. Darwin even suggests a model for how belief in spirits and gods could have arisen, using the behavior of his dog to underline the role of what are now called agency detection systems.[20] Darwin has a proto-religious dog, and he actually uses it to comment on how religious beliefs may ultimately have originated. So there is a kind of inspiration in Darwin for modern naturalistic accounts of the origins of religion.

Finally, I draw attention to one of the reasons why scholars still find Darwin deeply rewarding. This is because of his honesty and the nuances that he brings to his discussion. There is nearly always a complication, nearly always a qualification to his message. For example, in the letter to Asa Gray he considers a formula that might integrate both chance and design in the evolutionary process. The idea is that the laws may be designed but with the detailed outcomes left to chance. One finds oneself drawn into that interesting way of looking at things. And then one reads the next sentence. He has no sooner come up with that model than he says it does not at all satisfy him. In the letter to Fordyce, Darwin describes himself as having become increasingly agnostic in old age. Then he immediately adds "but not always." In fact "my beliefs often fluctuate." In his autobiography he wants to say that, in a suffering world, happiness decidedly prevails, and he even gives biological reasons why we might believe this. But then comes the qualification: how difficult this would be to prove! Finally, as in his autobiography, Darwin often expressed the conviction that this wonderful universe must have had a first cause. But even here we find an immediate qualification. Can we trust our own convictions if our minds are themselves limited products of evolution, ill equipped perhaps to solve metaphysical mysteries? There is a humility in Darwin that surely contrasts with the aggressive arrogance that we see in many of his disciples. There is also a transparent honesty. And it is these qualities that many have admired, irrespective of the religious beliefs they may or may not hold.

For Further Reflection

1. In the excerpt from Darwin's autobiography he summarizes, for members of his family, the reasons for his gradual rejection of Christianity. How great a role does he give to his scientific conclusions and in what ways did they contribute to his agnosticism?

2. In the same text Darwin devotes space to the problem of suffering, concluding tentatively that there is more happiness than misery in the world. At the same time he explains why the existence of so much suffering is consistent with his account of natural selection. In his writings he sometimes justifies his naturalistic theory by suggesting that it makes God less directly responsible for individual suffering and for specific features of creation, such as the egg-laying habits of the Ichneumon, that look more devilish than benign. Can we say that Darwin's theory provided new resources for theological engagement with the problem of pain and suffering?

3. In the same text Darwin identifies a recent scientific discovery that presents an "intolerable thought" because of the prospect of a "complete annihilation" of humankind. What are the most authentic Christian and Muslim responses today to this disclosure from the sciences?

4. What bearing, if any, does the possibility of giving an evolutionary account of the origins of religion have on the truth status of religious beliefs?

Notes

1. John Hedley Brooke, "Darwin and Victorian Christianity," in *The Cambridge Companion to Darwin*, eds. Jonathan Hodge and Gregory Radick, 2nd ed. (Cambridge: Cambridge University Press, 2009), 197–218; Luis Caruana, ed., *Darwin and Catholicism. The Past and Present Dynamics of a Cultural Encounter* (London: T & T Clark, 2009); Alister McGrath, *Darwinism and the Divine: Evolutionary Thought and Natural Theology* (Chichester: Wiley-Blackwell, 2011); James R. Moore, *The Post-Darwinian Controversies: A Study of the Protestant Struggle to Come to Terms with Darwin in Great Britain and America 1870–1900* (Cambridge: Cambridge University Press, 1979); Ronald L. Numbers, *The Creationists: From Scientific Creationism to Intelligent Design* (Cambridge, MA: Harvard University Press, 2006); and Jon H. Roberts, *Darwinism and the Divine in America: Protestant Intellectuals and Organic Evolution, 1859–1900* (Madison: University of Wisconsin Press, 1988).

2. Peter Harrison, *The Bible, Protestantism and the Rise of Natural Science* (Cambridge: Cambridge University Press, 1998), 169–84; and John Brooke and Geoffrey Cantor, *Reconstructing Nature: The Engagement of Science and Religion* (Edinburgh: T & T Clark, 1998), 141–243.

3. For recent discussions of this subject, see Celia Deane-Drummond and David Clough, eds., *Creaturely Theology* (London: SCM Press, 2009); and Michael J. Murray, *Nature Red in Tooth and Claw: Theism and the Problem of Animal Suffering* (Oxford: Oxford University Press, 2008).

4. For full biographical details, see Janet Browne, *Charles Darwin: Voyaging* (London: Pimlico, 1995), 36–144.

5. Charles Darwin, *The Correspondence of Charles Darwin*, ed. Frederick Burkhardt, vol. 7 (Cambridge: Cambridge University Press, 1991), 396–98, 403–4.

6. Frank J. Sulloway, "Darwin and His Finches: The Evolution of a Legend," *Journal of the History of Biology* 15 (1982): 1–53.

7. Adrian Desmond and James Moore, *Darwin* (London: Michael Joseph, 1991), 132–48.

8. John Hedley Brooke, " 'Laws Impressed on Matter by the Creator'? The *Origin* and the Question of Religion," in *The Cambridge Companion to the "Origin of Species,"* eds. Michael Ruse and Robert J. Richards (Cambridge: Cambridge University Press, 2009), 256–74.

9. Desmond and Moore, *Darwin*, 375–87; and Randal Keynes, *Annie's Box: Charles Darwin, His Daughter and Human Evolution* (London: Fourth Estate, 2001), 243–57.

10. Brooke, " 'Laws Impressed on Matter'?"; and David Kohn, "Darwin's Ambiguity: The Secularization of Biological Meaning," *British Journal for the History of Science* 22 (1989): 215–39.

11. Alvar Ellegård, *Darwin and the General Reader* (Stockholm: Almqvist and Wiksell, 1958); and John Rogerson, "What Difference Did Darwin Make? The Interpretation of Genesis in the Nineteenth Century," in *Reading Genesis after Darwin*, eds. Stephen C. Barton and David Wilkinson (Oxford: Oxford University Press, 2009), 75–91.

12. Darwin, *Correspondence*, vol. 8 (1993), 14.

13. For early reactions of Kingsley and Temple to advances in naturalistic explanation, see Darwin, *Correspondence*, vol. 7, 380; and Frederick Temple, *The Present Relations of Science to Religion* (Oxford: Parker, 1860).

14. Samuel Wilberforce, "Darwin's *Origin of Species*," in *Essays Contributed to the Quarterly Review*, vol. 1 (London: Murray, 1874), 52–103.

15. The many myths surrounding this famous encounter are exposed by David N. Livingstone in *Galileo Goes to Jail and Other Myths about Science and Religion*, ed. Ronald L. Numbers (Cambridge, MA: Harvard University Press, 2009), 152–69.

16. F. W. Farrar, *The Bible, Its Meaning and Supremacy* (London: Longmans, Green & Co, 1887), 154–56.

17. George J. Romanes, *Thoughts on Religion* (London: Longmans, Green & Co, 1896), 83.

18. David N. Livingstone, "Re-placing Darwinism and Christianity," in *When Science and Christianity Meet*, ed. David C. Lindberg and Ronald L. Numbers (Chicago: University of Chicago Press, 2003), 183–202.

19. Robert J. Richards, "Darwin's Theory of Natural Selection and Its Moral Purpose," in Richards and Ruse, *Cambridge Companion to the "Origin of Species,"* 47–66, especially 61.

20. Justin Barrett, *Why Would Anyone Believe in God?* (Lanham, MD: AltaMira Press, 2004).

Early Arabic Views of Darwin

MARWA ELSHAKRY

2009 MARKED BOTH THE 150TH ANNIVERSARY of Darwin's *Origin of Species* and the bicentennial of his birth. While most people today associate Darwin's name with that book, his most globally popular work by far for many decades was his 1871 *Descent of Man*—though it is now less widely read than *Origin* and many of the ideas it expresses (such as on race or on sexual selection) have had a much less successful afterlife than those of his earlier work. In fact, when I assign *Descent* in my classes, many of my students find themselves surprised by the contrast between the somewhat "outmoded" impression made on them by this work and their image of the Darwin who, despite his now two-hundred-year-old vintage, still lives among us in many ways as a kind of contemporary. Thanks largely to what some have called the "evolutionary synthesis" of the 1930s and the 1940s, which combined population genetics with natural selection, Darwin's theory of evolution helped to unify the disciplines of biology and has since been continuously reformulated in that context. This development also helped to purge his theory of what many increasingly saw as its "unacceptable metaphysical elements."[1] And yet the initial popularity of Darwin's *Descent* had been due to the fact that it was there that he finally made most explicit the implications of his theory for both metaphysics and morality.[2]

In the third chapter of *Descent*, from which the above passage is excerpted, Darwin laid out the "comparison of the mental powers of man and the lower animals" as part of his "evidence for the descent of man from some lower form." Among the powers he listed were the emotions, memory, imagination, reason, abstraction, language, sense of beauty and, finally, as Darwin puts it in the chapter index, "belief in God, spiritual agencies and superstitions." To demonstrate that "religion" was a "mental power" common to humans and animals, however, Darwin had to seriously rework the notion of religion itself.

128

He borrowed liberally from contemporary social thinkers (E. B. Tylor, John Lubbock, Herbert Spencer, and others), but I would argue that it was Darwin himself who did the most to radically reformulate the idea of religion in the modern world. What we find in these passages is the notion of religion as an abstract category—one that was cross-cultural, historically progressive, and universal (or, in Darwin's language, instinctual). Only thus could Darwin argue that it was in fact an evolutionary "mental power" or faculty common to all peoples.

It is precisely this aspect of *Descent* that provides us with a key explanation for Darwin's early sensational popularity, both within the Western Christian tradition and beyond it. Yet the idea that faiths could evolve and be considered comparatively, and potentially hierarchically, from a naturalistic perspective—as in from "fetishism" to "polytheism" and ultimately to "monotheism" (as described in the last paragraph of the excerpt)—held a potentially highly subversive message from the point of view of religious faith, for it could allow you to argue for the radical contingency of belief in general. This was how Shiblī Shumayyil, for instance, interpreted Darwin's views. Shumayyil (1850–1917) was a lapsed Catholic who was educated in Protestant missionary schools in Ottoman Beirut and was among the first and most influential writers to popularize Darwin's ideas in the Arabic-speaking Muslim world. He was also heavily influenced by German materialism: like many Ottoman intellectuals at the time, he read Darwin's theory of evolution through the lens of Ludwig Büchner and Ernst Haeckel. Shumayyil's main opus was, in fact, a translation of Büchner's commentaries on Darwin. That he chose to translate Büchner rather than Darwin was deliberate because he felt it completed Darwin's vision and drew the proper materialistic conclusions from it.[3] But, as we will see, Shumayyil came under attack from many sides for what many felt was a rather distorted version of Darwin's own ideas. In short, the arguments elicited by Shumayyil suggest that there remained a kind of fundamental ambiguity in Darwin's treatment of the question of religion. In reflecting on these passages, therefore, it is useful to consider how Darwin defines "religion," and in particular how we might think of the novelty of his definition vis-à-vis earlier treatments, whether they be scriptural or scholastic, and how this definition might differ from a view of religion that is embodied in both practice and discourse—in other words, a view of religion that involves a historically evolving set of discourses rather than, say, inherited instincts.[4]

As for the letters and the autobiography, the central issue they raise is the question of natural theology. In a letter to Asa Gray and in his posthumously published autobiography, Darwin claims that it was the problem of suffering in nature that led him to question the emphasis on design and beneficence in the classical model of natural theology (a model familiar and initially congenial to him from his student days in Cambridge). Now the relation of natural theology to natural selection is a complex subject that could be discussed at great length. But I want to focus specifically on the question of suffering that this letter raises and in particular to think about the role of theodicy in the construction of theologies of nature in both Christianity and Islam. For instance, few of Darwin's Muslim readers pick up on the question of either human suffering or the problem of evil in the natural order of things. Indeed, while this issue occasionally comes up in contemporary discussions of medical ethics in relation to human illness and disease, it is much less prevalent on the whole in Muslim discussions of the nonhuman natural world. Once again, this is a vast topic that I can only touch upon here—and one that may ultimately relate to the construction of variant theologies of death (or pain)—yet my question in this regard is somewhat more circumscribed: namely, what are the practical implications of these divergences in the place of theodicy vis-à-vis views of nature for discussions of virtue in the various discursive traditions within both Christianity and Islam?

Another aspect of this letter also deserves our attention. Despite his melancholic reflections on the idea of divinely ordained laws that could lead to homicidal lightning bolts and idiot children, at the end of his letter to Gray (who was sometimes labeled by his contemporaries a "theistic evolutionist"), Darwin wrote: "I can see no reason, why a man, or other animal, may not have been aboriginally produced by other laws; & that all these laws may have been expressly designed by an omniscient Creator, who foresaw every future event & consequence." Similarly in his autobiography, he admits that when he wrote *Origin* he felt "compelled to look to a First Cause"—though he also earlier noted how the "very old argument from the existence of suffering against the existence of an intelligent first cause seems to me a strong one" and concludes that "the mystery of the beginning of all things is insoluble by us."

Despite all these qualifications, Darwin's own references to the possibility and at times to the necessity of a First Cause were readily picked up by his readers. This was the case with Ismāʿīl Maẓhar, who was the first to provide an Arabic translation of *Origin* in 1918 (although he only published the first five chapters then, adding four more in 1928). Maẓhar was a largely self-educated Egyptian Muslim, a prolific translator, and important literary figure who died in 1962. In many ways his own religious outlook is as difficult to pinpoint as Darwin's. Nevertheless, Maẓhar remained a committed evolutionist through-out his long literary career, and he often argued against the view that subscrib-ing to evolution challenged faith in a personal God. He was also a sharp critic of Shumayyil's materialistic version of Darwin as well as of what he thought was a kind of caricatured critique of evolution by Muslim writers such as Jamāl al-Dīn al-Afghānī.[5]

Maẓhar, like Darwin, saw no reason why one could not hold on to a belief in the absolute regularity of nature and of natural laws as well as to the idea of a First Cause in nature, but he also cautioned that science could only really deal with the chain of relations between manifest appearances as expressed in natural laws and not with actual or real causes. Arguing loosely from both Kant and al-Ghazālī, he also thought that one could not ultimately attain knowledge of God as a real or actual existence in and of itself any more than one can attain knowledge of the external world beyond the mind's compre-hension. A kind of transcendental positivist or neopositivist in a Spencerian vein, Maẓhar also reversed the flow of skepticism that had typically moved from the postpositivist sciences to theology by arguing that even the modern sciences relied on ontological categories that must be believed in but that can-not be known by science (categories such as the existence of a world outside ourselves, the persistence of force, a belief in scientific causation and so forth). Like Spencer, he referred to the concept of the Unknowable as a means of avoiding any metaphysical commitment to the nature of reality: arguing that the true natures of space, time, matter, motion, and force were "absolutely incomprehensible." But Spencer's vague deferring of ontological questions via a position of epistemological skepticism has fallen out of fashion. Another topic for further reflection, therefore, is whether questions of first or ultimate causes can really be posed in reference to the modern sciences today, and, if so, if they necessarily entail the same kind of epistemological bifurcation that they did in the past?

One final point in connection with Maẓhar's treatment of Darwin: while many people across both the evolutionist and creationist divide associate Dar-win's naturalistic philosophy with religious skepticism, what the example of

Maẓhar shows, I think, is that Darwin in fact served as much as a force for religious resurgence of a kind as a force for skepticism. Just as Darwin's thought allowed people like Maẓhar to formulate questions about the nature of the boundaries of knowledge in Islam, it led others such as the key late-nineteenth-century theologian Muḥammad 'Abduh to revive interest in Ibn Rushd's views on causality and spurred the Sufi scholar Ḥusayn al-Jisr to clarify a modern Ash'arite view of *tafsīr* or exegesis. In fact, the very organization of this seminar could itself be said to illustrate the point.

For Further Reflection

1. How does Darwin refer to "religion"? In what ways does this reflect or differ from conceptions of faith in other texts in this volume?

2. Much of Darwin's thinking on natural selection was informed by Anglican natural theology—in fact, in some ways his theory could be said merely to have stood William Paley's *Natural Theology* on its head. As such, much of his reflection on the moral valuation of nature deals with questions of beneficence and suffering in nature. Would these ideas have the same significance in traditions where theologies of nature were decoupled from questions of theodicy? What is the resonance of these ideas among modern Muslim thinkers for instance? And what are the implications of these divergences for conceptions of nature itself?

3. Although he sometimes fluctuated on the point, Darwin often made room for the possibility of a First Cause in nature in many of his personal and published writings. This was an idea that was readily taken up by many of his readers in the past, particularly by both Christian and Muslim evolutionists. Does this question hold the same sort of significance today? And what are the epistemological, ontological, and methodological stakes involved?

4. Much of Darwin's theory of evolution by natural selection deals with the competition or "struggle for life." But what of death itself? In other words, what meaning or significance does death have for Darwin? How might that compare with particular moral philosophies in the various discursive traditions of Islam and Christianity? And does his view of the evolution of humanity's "moral faculties"—which he touches upon in the selections from *Descent of Man*—leave room for these?

Notes

1. Vassiliki Betty Smocovitis, *Unifying Biology: The Evolutionary Synthesis and Evolutionary Biology* (Princeton, NJ: Princeton University Press, 1996), 100.

2. For more on this, see Robert Richards, "Darwin on Mind, Morals, and Emotions," in *The Cambridge Companion to Darwin*, eds. J. Hodge and G. Radick (Cambridge: Cambridge University Press, 2003), 92–115.

3. On Shiblī Shumayyil, see his *Ta'rīb li-Sharḥ Buḵhnir 'alā madhhab Dārwīn fī intiqāl al-anwā' wa-ẓuhūr al-'ālam al-'uḍwī wa-iṭlāq dhālika 'alā al-insān ma'a ba'ḍ taṣarruf fīh* (al-Iskandarīyah: Maṭbat'at Jarīdat al-Maḥrūsah, 1884), and *Falsafat al-nushū' wa-irtiqā'* (Miṣr: Maṭ-ba'at al-Muqtaṭaf, 1910); also Georges Haroun, *Šiblī Šumayyil: Une pensée évolutionniste Arabe à l'époque d'an-Nahda* (Beirut: Publications de l'Université Libanaise, 1985). On Ottoman materialists, see M. Şükrü Hanioğlu, "Blueprint for a Future Society: Late Ottoman Materialists on Science, Religion and Art," in Elisabeth Ozdalga, *Late Ottoman Society: The Intellectual Legacy* (London: Routledge, 2005), 28–116.

4. The idea that we might recalibrate this modernist notion of religion from a social and historically embodied perspective is one that anthropologists of religion such as Talal Asad have dealt with extensively. See Talal Asad, *Genealogies of Religion: Disciplines and Reasons of Power in Islam and Christianity* (Baltimore: Johns Hopkins University Press, 1993); and Ovamir Anjum, "Islam as a Discursive Tradition: Talal Asad and His Interlocutors," *Comparative Studies of South Asia, Africa and the Middle East* 27, no. 3 (2007): 656–72.

5. On Ismā'īl Maẓhar, see his translation of the first nine chapters of *Origin of Species*, *Aṣl al-anwā' wa-nushū'ihā bi-al-intikhāb al-ṭabī'ī; wa-ḥifẓ al-ṣufūf al-ghālibah fī al-tanāḥur 'alā al-baqā'* (Cairo: Dār al-'Aṣr lil-Ṭab' wa-al-Nashr, 1928); and *Malqā al-sabīl fī madhhab al-nushū' wa-al-irtiqā' wa-athāruhu fī al-fikr al-ḥadīth* (Miṣr: al-Maṭba'ah, 1926).

Modern Islamic Texts

Sayyid Quṭb, commentary on Qur'ān 2:189

THEY ASK YOU about the new moon; say, "They are means people use for measuring time, and for Pilgrimage." Righteousness does not mean that you enter houses from the rear, but truly righteous is he who fears God. Enter dwellings by their [front] doors and fear God, so that you may prosper. [Qur'ān 2:189]

The significance of the new moon may be viewed in more than one way. Some reports suggest that the Prophet Muḥammad was asked why the moon goes through its various phases. Others say that he was asked why the new moon appears in such a regular fashion, which would have been more consistent with the answer given in the *sūrah*: *"They are means people use for measuring time, and for the Pilgrimage."*

They serve as a means by which people fix and measure the time of important religious and worldly events and activities such as travel, Pilgrimage, fasting, marriage and divorce, as well as trade transactions and loan periods.

Whatever the original enquiry, the answer had gone beyond mere abstraction and given practical, rather than "scientific," information relating to the phases of the moon. The Qur'ān, without going into a detailed astronomical discussion, spoke of the function of the moon and its role in people's daily life. Despite its being implied in the question, the Qur'ān did not embark on an explanation of the moon's position within the solar system or the relative movement of stars, planets and galaxies.

What significance lies behind the answer given by the Qur'ān?

The Qur'ān's principal objective was the creation and promotion of a new conception of life in a new social, political and economic order. Indeed, it was working towards the creation of a new human community, with a special role of leadership in the world. It was developing a new model of human society, the like of which had not been known before, to uphold a new way of life that would firmly establish essential universal features and principles which the rest of mankind would look up to and emulate.

A "scientific" answer would undoubtedly have provided the Prophet's followers with theoretical knowledge about the universe, to add to their meagre understanding of it. Indeed, it is doubtful that the Arabs knew enough about astronomy at that time to be able to make use of further theoretical information, which would have required an understanding of basic principles and phenomena that were beyond all scientific progress achieved in the world up to that time.

The Qur'ān avoided a "scientific" answer because people were not ready for it, and it would have been of little use for the universal mission the Qur'ān was revealed to fulfil. Its role was far greater than the mere dissemination of detailed knowledge. The Qur'ān was never intended to be a book on astronomy, chemistry or medicine, as some of its admirers and detractors try, each for their own different purposes, to demonstrate.

These attempts betray a lack of understanding of the nature of the Qur'ān, and of its function and scope. It is mainly concerned with the human soul and the state and direction of the human condition. Its purpose is to establish a broad view of the world in which we exist and its relationship with the Creator, and with a general outline of man's position in this world and his relationship with the Creator. On the basis of these broad concepts, the Qur'ān goes on to establish a way of life which enables man to apply all his skills and abilities, not least his intellectual faculties. Once these are properly and correctly developed, they are given full freedom, through observation, experiment and scientific research, to probe the mysteries of life and the Universe and make the appropriate conclusions—which could never, in any case, be said to be final or absolute.

The basic raw material with which the Qur'ān is concerned is man himself: the way he views things around him, his beliefs, emotions and ideas, his behaviour and activity, and the ties and relationships that govern his life. The conduct and development of material science and innovation are left to man's mental and intellectual capabilities and his diligent endeavour to know and understand. It is this knowledge and understanding that are the essential prerequisites for man to fulfil his Divinely-ordained mission in the world, for which he is naturally fitted and qualified.

The Qur'ān nurtures man's basic nature and protects it against deviation and corruption. It provides man with the moral, social, political and economic foundations and mechanisms that enable him to put his talents and skills to full and proper use. It furnishes him with a broad and comprehensive view of nature, the inherent harmony, and the delicate balance of the physical world, of which man himself is an important and integral part, and its relationship with the Creator.

The Qur'ān does not cover such topics in great detail, because that is man's task. He is expected to take the initiative to search, discover and use his environment in order to further and fulfil his supreme position in the world.

The attempt to make the Qur'ān what it was never meant to be often seems naïve and counter-productive. The fact that the Qur'ān is not a reference book for medicine or chemistry or astronomy takes nothing away from its power and glory.

The Qur'ān deals with something much wider and more comprehensive than all those sciences. It is concerned with man himself, the key to uncovering the facts and mysteries of the world around. The human mind is fully equipped to scrutinise and probe into man's surroundings, and to experiment with and apply the theories he formulates and the tools he invents. The Qur'ān concentrates on nurturing man's character, conscience and mind, and laying the sound foundations of the human environment which allows him to make full use of his own hidden potential and that of the world around. Having laid down the groundwork and given man the necessary mental tools and criteria, the Qur'ān leaves man free to seek and search, experiment, achieve and make mistakes, in all areas of life.

There is also a great risk in attempting to seek verification of facts of a scientific nature given occasionally in the Qur'ān through suppositions, theories or so-called "scientific facts" arrived at through human empirical efforts.

The facts that the Qur'ān mentions are absolute and final truths, while those arrived at through human research are not, no matter how advanced or sophisticated the means or the approach used to arrive at them. The latter are constrained by the conditions of man's own environment, and they are limited by the nature and scope of the tools used. The absolute and final truths of the Qur'ān cannot, therefore, be qualified or authenticated by the inconclusive ones discovered by man.

In addition to "scientific fact," this applies in the case of "scientific theory." This includes theories on the origin of the universe, the creation and evolution of man, and psychological and sociological theories. Even within the realm of human thought, these are not considered to express scientific facts. Indeed, they are no more than suppositions or speculative ideas which, at best, help explain a vast array of physical, biological, psychological or sociological phenomena. As more accurate instruments and more discoveries are made, these theories are constantly amended and developed, or superseded by others that give wider or more accurate explanations or interpretations.

The attempt to verify Qur'ānic facts by the changing findings of human science is fundamentally flawed. It reflects three negative aspects that should not be associated with the Qur'ān.

First is an inner defeatism that science is somehow superior to the Qur'ān, whose facts and principles need no verification or corroboration. But in fact, Qur'ānic statements are definitive, complete and conclusive, while human science remains in a constant state of flux and development. This is due to the constraints of the environment in which human research and experiment are conducted, and the inadequacy of the tools and methods used in those processes.

Second is a misunderstanding of the true nature and function of the Qur'ān as the absolute definitive truth addressing man in his totality according to his basic nature and within the constraints of the physical world and its laws. Ideally, it aims to achieve perfect harmony between man and the physical world, avoiding a clash between man and nature and enabling him, through enquiry, observation, experiment and application to unravel as many of the world's mysteries as he can and use its potential energies and resources to enhance his position and role as God's representative on Earth.

Third is the continuous interpretation and re-interpretation, with frequent resort to involved and fantastic methods, of Qur'ānic statements in a vain attempt to make them agree or coincide with speculative suppositions and tentative theories.

However, this should not prevent us from making full use of what human sciences uncover about man, life and the world, for a better understanding of the Qur'ān. God says: *"We shall show them [people] Our signs across all corners of the world and within themselves, until they clearly see that it [the Qur'ān] is the truth"* (Fuṣṣilat 41:53). This is a clear call to study closely and absorb what science discovers of God's signs and to use them to expand the meaning and application of the Qur'ānic injunctions, without undermining or demeaning the immutability and integrity of the Qur'ān.

This may be illustrated further by the following examples.

The Qur'ān says: *"And He created all things and ordained them in due proportion"* (al-Furqān 25:2). Scientific observation also has led to the conclusion that there are inherent harmony, very intricate interactions and consonances within the structure of the universe. The earth's shape and distance from both the sun and the moon, its size relative to theirs, its speed and axis of rotation, and countless other factors combine to make life on Earth possible and sustainable. None of this may be attributed to chance or coincidence, or can be said to be without purpose.

These observations no doubt are useful in gaining a better understanding of the Qur'ānic statement. This is quite legitimate and should be encouraged.

The Qur'ān says: *"We [God] created man from an extraction of clay"* (al-Mu'-minūn 23:12). Centuries later, scientists such as Charles Darwin proposed a theory of evolution, which purports that life began in water as a single cell, and that human beings are the result of millions of years of evolution. Now, it would be pointless, indeed wrong, to attempt to show that this is precisely what the Qur'ān said.

To begin with, the theory is not conclusive and, within a century, it has undergone several amendments and changes that have made it almost unrecognisable. There were flaws in the original theory which was conceived at a time when nothing was known of the genes which carry hereditary properties and distinguish one species from another. Several aspects of Darwin's theory have since been disproved, and many others are still a matter of debate.

The Qur'ānic statement establishes the origin of man without giving any details of the process itself. It does not aim at more than that and carries no other connotations or meaning.

The Qur'ān tells us: *"And the sun speeds towards its resting place"* (Yā Sīn 36:38). This is a statement of fact. Science has shown us the sun is indeed moving relative to other stars nearby and is part of a galaxy which itself is moving. Such measurements, relative and inconclusive as they are, do not affect the truth of the Qur'ānic statement, which is final.

The Qur'ān says: *"Are the unbelievers unaware that the heavens and the earth were but one solid mass and We split them asunder?"* (al-Anbiyā' 21:30). Some have tried to reconcile this statement with the so-called "Big Bang" theory, which claims that the universe exploded from a single point. It is futile to try and limit Qur'ānic statements with human scientific theory. The "Big Bang" theory is not the only one in its fields and it is contested by many scientists, while the Qur'ānic statement is complete and conclusive. It merely states a fact without telling us what is meant by "heavens" or how the fragmentation occurred. No scientific proposition should be used to corroborate Qur'ānic statements, no matter how close or similar the conclusions may be.[1]

Shaykh Muḥammad Mitwallī al-Shaʿrāwī: "The Qur'ān and the Universe"

Since the initial revelation, the meanings within the Qur'ān have maintained relevance despite science's latest discoveries and theories, giving credibility to some and refuting others.

Regarding the Qur'ān and scientific theories, it might be useful to draw attention to the unsound and hazardous attempts by some overzealous students who make use of scientific theories to confirm the recorded facts found in the Qur'ān or to enhance its authenticity. No less dangerous than this attitude is the practice by some scientists and scholars who attempt to elucidate the Qur'ān in terms of these scientific discoveries or ascribe to some verses and facts the power of foretelling future events, only to be stunned later by discovering that they have been over-enthusiastic. Many have overlooked the indisputable fact that the credibility of the Qur'ān does not depend upon evidence from science or any other field of knowledge. The Qur'ān should not be regarded as a scientific text, but rather as Scripture with a system of discipline for leading a virtuous life, decreed by Allah for the benefit and welfare of mankind.

Allah, however, knew that in the course of time there would emerge sceptics who would proclaim the decline of the age of divine power and herald their allegiance to the power of science. To foil this impious misconception, Allah supported the Qur'ān with many scientific facts about the universe and its organisation which no one else but He knew at the time of the Qur'ān's revelation.

The following verse, whose meaning has remained hidden for centuries, has only recently begun to yield its wealth of scientific data. This happened when mankind became able to assimilate such complex knowledge.

"We shall show them Our portents on the horizons and within themselves until it be manifest unto them that it is the Truth . . ." (Fuṣṣilat 41:53)

It is important to draw the reader's attention to the future tense of the verb "show." Actually the verse refers to the endless future; it addresses not only the present age or the one that follows, but rather the whole of mankind from now until eternity.

This regeneration of meaning and its inexhaustibility should not, however, be used as a justification to ascribe to the verses any meaning other than what they presently yield. We should approach the Qur'ān as a divine message that has come to provide us with knowledge about this world and organise our relationship with it and with its Creator. It has not come to reveal the fundamental laws of geometry, architecture, astronomy or any other science. In fact, Allah defines the Qur'ān's fundamental objective in the first verse of the Surah "the Cow," in which He says:

"That is the Scripture whereof there is no doubt, a guidance to all those who ward off (evil)." (al-Baqarah 2:2)

Although the Qur'ān is primarily a scripture of guidance and worship, Allah has recorded in it factual knowledge capable of answering and clarifying any misconceptions that might arise in the course of time. Some revelations which touch upon scientific phenomena have not completely unfolded. All of them, however, are meant to discredit those heretics who hail the doctrine of science and decry the doctrine of faith and who, in their foolish and misguided conceit, have been oblivious of the fact that science, to which they vow allegiance, is of Allah's own making. It is He alone who unfolds the secrets of science to mankind when He wills. This knowledge which has been imparted to man should not be used to validate the Qur'ān.

The Qur'ān can prove or disprove the findings of science, but it is safer and wiser to refrain from correlating any scientific theory with the facts recorded in it until it has been proved and verified beyond any doubt. It is grievously wrong to hastily attribute something to Allah, only to discover, later, that it is untrue. All scientific hypotheses which disagree with the Qur'ān have been proved to be unfounded and lacking in empirical evidence.

It is often asked why the Qur'ān did not elucidate the scientific facts recorded in its verses to those who were alive at the time of its revelation, or to the generation who followed them. Indeed, the scientific knowledge and facts recorded in the Qur'ān involve universal phenomena which have a significant bearing on man's survival, regardless of how they function. Thus the energy of the sun, the earth's gravity and its rotation day and night, the development of the embryo and all similar phenomena are created to serve man and ensure his survival on earth. He need not be fully acquainted with the details of how they function in order to benefit from their useful properties.

There are millions who know nothing about the physiological processes of conception and pregnancy, yet this lack of knowledge does not stop them from having children. Similarly, there are millions who do not know that the sun is the main source of life on earth, and yet enjoy all the benefits derived from this distant star. Hence there was no urgent necessity, at that early stage, to explain these complex scientific phenomena to those who lived at the time of the revelation of the Qur'ān and the generation who followed them. They were given as much as their intellect could assimilate, in proportion to the growth of that intellect.

There have been those who have contended that some of the facts recorded in the Qur'ān diverge widely from the empirically validated laws of science. This contention is both misleading and inaccurate. In fact, disagreement can arise only when the verses are either misinterpreted and their true meaning not understood, or when an unproved scientific hypothesis is exploited to inveigh against the Qur'ān. It is, therefore, safer and wiser to refrain from using science to justify Qur'ānic facts because the Qur'ān, though higher than human knowledge, was not meant to be a reference to assess the validity of scientific discoveries. . . .[2]

. . . The Qur'ān has touched upon many facts about life and human existence which science has only recently discovered. Some of these facts are extremely intricate and were little known to past generations. Neither Muḥammad nor anyone else could have attributed such facts to the work of Allah unless they were truly His, for had they proved to be inaccurate or false the credibility of the message, as well as that of the Messenger, would have been destroyed. It would be naive to suggest that Muḥammad (SAW) was unaware of this possibility, and one would have expected him to avoid such matters if he had had the slightest doubt about their source and truth. Why would he have broached such matters of which he had no knowledge and which until recently have remained part of the knowledge confined to Allah?

It is indeed remarkable to compare what Allah revealed to Muḥammad some fourteen hundred years ago concerning the embryo, with the most recent scientific discoveries in the field of embryology:

> "Verily We created man from a product of wet earth: then placed him as a drop (of seed) in a safe lodging; then fashioned We the drop a clot, then fashioned We the clot a little lump, then fashioned We the little lump bones, then clothed the bones with flesh, and then produced it as another creation. So blessed be Allah, the Best of Creators." (al-Mu'minūn 23:12–14)[3]

Notes

1. Sayyid Quṭb, *In the Shade of the Qur'ān*, vol. 1 (Leicester: Islamic Foundation, 1999), 199–204.

2. Shaykh Muḥammad Mitwallī al-Shaʿrāwī, *The Miracles of the Qur'ān* (London: Dar al-Taqwa, 1989), 65–68.

3. Ibid., 72.

Introduction to Quṭb
and al-Shaʿrāwī

SHERINE HAMDY

Sayyid Quṭb (1906–66)

THE TEXT CHOSEN IS AN EXCERPT from Quṭb's thirty-volume *tafsīr* (exegesis) of the Qurʾān, which he wrote over a fifteen-year period, most of which was spent inside Nasser's political prisons in the 1950s and 1960s. Quṭb is today mostly known as a political ideologue of the Muslim Brotherhood. Recently, he has figured in the US media as the man who provided the seeds of thought for the extremists of al-Qaeda (particularly in his writings about his life in America, where he traveled as a student). Yet whatever genealogical links contemporary extremists might claim to Quṭb, it is important to reflect lucidly and with some critical distance on the importance of his writings, which remain tremendously influential throughout the contemporary Muslim world. His corpus of writing cannot be reduced to his political manifestos, which—it should be remembered, in any case—were written in the context of being persecuted and brutally tortured in prison for opposing Nasser's autocratic socialist regime.

Sayyid Quṭb was born in 1906 in the Upper Egyptian village of Musha in Asyut, where he was raised by a devout family, and he had memorized the Holy Qurʾān by the age of ten. After years of imprisonment, Quṭb was executed by Nasser's regime in 1966, on charges that he had conspired against the state. These charges were based on the political views that he expressed in his book *Milestones*, in which he sanctioned violence as a means to overthrow unjust rule. Many contemporary Muslims consider him to have died a martyr (*shahīd*) at the hands of a dictator.

Quṭb's *tafsīr* has remained influential throughout the Muslim world. In the excerpt we have here, Quṭb writes that the Qurʾān did not give a detailed astronomical or scientific answer to the questions posed to the Prophet Muḥammad (peace and blessings be upon him) about the new moon. He writes that the Qur'ān "was never intended to be a book on astronomy, chemistry or medicine, as some of its admirers and detractors try, each for their own different purposes, to demonstrate."[1]

In stating that the Qur'ān was not a book of science, Quṭb was responding to a trend, most famously and influentially solidified by the Egyptian reformer and theologian Muḥammad 'Abduh in the late nineteenth century. Taken aback by European ascendance and colonial subordination of Muslim lands, 'Abduh saw science as the key to modern power. 'Abduh felt that unless Muslims emphasized the compatibility of reason and scientific knowledge with the aims and goals of religion, Islam would become irrelevant to the ordinary Muslim. In his reformation of al-Azhar, 'Abduh often stated: "Those who claim that science and reason have nothing to do with religion are ignorant of the true principles of Islam."[2] Science and rationality, for 'Abduh, led to better Muslim practice; conversely, Islam's emphasis on reason, proof, and evidence helped cultivate a disposition toward scientific enquiry. According to 'Abduh, the Qur'ān could never contradict scientific evidence, and nothing in science could be found to contradict the Qur'ān. 'Abduh made references to scientific topics at the time in his new approach to *tafsīr*: for example, he postulated that microscopic entities could be seen as *jinn*, and pointed to embryological developments described in the Qur'ān as corresponding to those published in scientific journals. 'Abduh's audience included the *'ulamā'* at al-Azhar, who were averse to looking outside their arcane texts and suspicious of the outside world.

Half a century later, the works of Sayyid Quṭb emerged in a rather different social reality. In contrast to 'Abduh, who argued that science was a legitimate form of knowledge against those who saw the Qur'ān as the sole source of truth, Quṭb's position was to argue for the enduring authority of the Qur'ān against those who felt that modern science had rendered it obsolete. Writing in the mid-1950s, Quṭb felt an urgent need to defend Islam in the face of the rapid changes wrought by modernization, materialism, and secularism. While his writings encompass such different topics as literary criticism, Islam's relation to capitalism and communism, social justice, Qur'ānic exegesis, and commentaries on Western materialism, a consistent theme in Quṭb's writings is "the usurpation of divine authority, the unhappy condition in which humanity found itself as a consequence, and the project of reinstating divine authority as the only way of restoring humanity to a state of happiness."[3] Throughout his works Quṭb decries the usurpation of divine authority by humans, more specifically, by modern Muslims who marginalize and persecute the less powerful. In this way he voiced his political views about social injustice and illegitimate rule through theological arguments about divine sovereignty. The consolidation of modern state power enabled the new Egyptian state to exert social and political control to a degree Muslims had never before experienced. This led Quṭb to state that the sort of hegemony that the state claimed for itself could not be tolerated in Islam, for only God could possess such authority.[4]

This political context informed Quṭb's assertion of the limits of human knowledge as well as the epistemology that he developed with respect to science and the Qur'ān. Just as human beings could not administer life without the guidance of God, so too they could not pretend to know about the truth of God's creation in formulations of science. According to Quṭb, there are limits to human knowledge and to the fields in which humans could appropriately inquire. One of these fields of knowledge that will (and should) remain with God alone involves the question of divine will and human ability to act within that will.

Quṭb thus drew a sharp line between the realm of the human and the realm of the divine: the Qur'ān—reflecting divine knowledge—was the eternal guidance for this world and the next, while human knowledge, in contrast, was necessarily temporal, inconstant, imperfect, and inferior to the truth of God. He argued that attempts to corroborate imperfect human knowledge with the eternal truth of the Qur'ān were incorrect, for to do so implied that science had an equal authority to scripture. Further, Quṭb clarified that the purposes of the Qur'ān and the realm of science were entirely different and could not be considered as parallel categories for analysis. Quṭb was weary of Muslims constantly apologizing for Islam and twisting history and scripture to make them conform to science. According to Quṭb, science is the mere dissemination of detailed knowledge and pales in comparison to the lofty mission of the Qur'ān, which was sent as a guidance and indeed salvation for all of mankind as spiritual beings and vice-regents (*al-insān al-mukhallaf*) for God on earth. If ever scientific ideas appear to be in conflict with the Qur'ān, Quṭb insists that our impulse as Muslims should not be to bend and twist the verses apologetically to have them conform; rather, we should recognize that science, as a human product, is necessarily imperfect and changes with time. By its nature, then, it should not be placed, either categorically or comparatively, alongside the truth of God.

Shaykh al-Shaʿrāwī (1911–98)

Shaykh Muḥammad Mutwallī al-Shaʿrāwī was born in the Egyptian village of Daqadous in 1911 and died in 1998. It would be difficult to overstate the significance of his role in religious revivalism in Egypt and neighboring countries. Unlike Quṭb, whose writings were translated into other non-Arabic languages and read in non-Arab Muslim countries, Shaʿrāwī's influence is mostly felt in the Arabic-speaking Muslim world. This is because most people encounter Shaʿrāwī's words orally, through his telegenic performances, not through his writing. Shaʿrāwī was well known for his television shows, *Nūr ʿalā nūr* (Light Upon Light) and *Khawāṭir īmāniyya* (Faithful Steps), in which he gave weekly sermons and commentaries on the Qurʾān, making its language and meanings accessible, attractive, and beautiful to everyday believers.

Shaʿrāwī's unrivaled command of the Arabic language, coupled with his inimitable bodily gestures, made him a most beloved figure, particularly throughout Egypt. He was in political exile during Nasser's regime, but Sadat, seeking to consolidate his power against his Nasserist critics, welcomed Shaʿrāwī back to Egypt, appointed him as minister of religious endowments, and eventually gave him his own slot on national television. Writing in the 1990s, the Danish scholar Jakob Skovgaard-Petersen mused that he would often enter the homes of first-generation literate friends in Egypt to find two books: the Qurʾān and a compendium of Shaʿrāwī's fatwas.[5]

Shaʿrāwī's talent was to make the Qurʾānic message appear relevant and accessible to everyday Muslims living under the exigencies of modern life. He constantly spoke against the assumption that new technologies make Islamic teachings outdated or irrelevant. In one of the compendia of Shaʿrāwī's teachings, he responded to the question: "How is it that the Qurʾān claims that God alone knows what is in mothers' wombs, when we today have ultrasound technology?" His reply was that we may now know things like the sex of the fetus, but only God knows the fate and future life of the child to come. In responding to another questioner, he explained that by "making test-tube babies" scientists were not creating life but were rather only facilitating a process that God, the sole Creator, had already created; this was the same reply he gave later when asked about cloning.[6] Unlike muftis in state-appointed positions who often worked to facilitate the aims of the state by judging medical interventions to be "beneficial" and "permissible," Shaʿrāwī frequently voiced opinions against particular types of medical interventions in the context of telling believing, pious Muslims that they need not fear death and reminding them that the Qurʾān bears the ultimate truth.[7] He often criticized both the views of those who considered the Qurʾān outdated and the arguments of those seeking to prove the authenticity of the Qurʾān by appealing to its "scientific miracles."

In the excerpt included in this volume, Shaʿrāwī writes: "Since the initial revelation, the meanings within the Qurʾān have maintained relevance despite science's latest discoveries and theories, giving credibility to some and refuting others."[8] Shaʿrāwī here stresses that it is the Qurʾān that remains the arbiter of truth: the Qurʾān's message stays eternal and true while scientific theories might come and go. At the same time, Shaʿrāwī later makes reference, as did ʿAbduh, to the Qurʾān's anticipation of developments in modern embryology, and other scientific advances.[9] Is Shaʿrāwī's reference to embryology, then, a contradiction? Why does he say that we should not try to prove the Qurʾān's authenticity by pointing to its parallels with science while at other times he appears to be doing just that? I will briefly make two points to elucidate this apparent puzzle.

First, Shaʿrāwī's seemingly contradictory statements involve different uses of the term "science"; these different uses of the term also explain the seemingly contrasting views of ʿAbduh and Quṭb. When Shaʿrāwī, following ʿAbduh, describes science's concordance with the Qurʾān, he means by science that which has gained the status of self-evident truth. Yet when, like Quṭb, he claims that science and the Qurʾān should not be compared with one another, he is thinking of science as a human institution practiced by fallible and socially situated scientists. Shaʿrāwī's audience was composed of people who were in many cases better informed about the arguments and reasoning of modern science than about Islamic teachings. His focus on Qurʾānic language was part of his larger role as a *dāʿiya*, or caller to Islam. Shaʿrāwī was willing to draw on the language of science—the everyday, the mundane—to inspire awe in his followers about the magnificence of the Qurʾān. As a *dāʿiya*, he was expected to be conversant with the language and thinking of those to whom he sought to reach out, in this case, their indoctrination by the idea of modern science as purveyor of truth. Whereas he agrees with Qutb that human understanding of scientific truth is necessarily imperfect and temporal and therefore irrelevant to the true meaning of the Qur'ān, Sha'rāwī also maintains that humans could use what little truth they thought they knew to shed light on the Qur'ān and on what he often called its "oceans of meanings."

Second, when Sha'rāwī states that science should not be used to validate the Qur'ān, he means that science should not hold a higher status in relation to the truth than the Qur'ān. Here he is distancing himself from endeavors such as those of the Commission on Scientific Signs of Qur'ān and Sunnah of the Muslim World League, founded in 1984. Zaghloul el-Naggar, chairman of this commission, holds that scientific knowledge can help decode Qur'ānic verses and vice versa, the ultimate goal being to uncover a higher truth. Working from a materialistic-scientific framework, members of this commission understand the heavens in terms of gaseous phases and the six days of Creation in terms of stages of the elements that coincide with the relative age of the universe and of the planet, as determined by astronomers, astrophysicists, and geologists. This approach to the relationship between the Qur'ān and science, with its popular website and satellite television shows dedicated to the Qur'ān's "scientific miracles," has a great following throughout the Muslim world.[10] As Marwa Elshakry writes, referring to this type of approach: "For millions of Muslims around the world today . . . scientific exegesis continues to provide the means to demonstrate the modernity as well as the comprehensiveness" of Islam.[11]

Such an approach as that of el-Naggar is distinct from that of Qutb, who held that the details of creation constitute knowledge that belongs to God alone, and from that of Sha'rāwī, who held that whatever humans could glean from science should serve the purpose of illuminating the Qur'ān's vast meanings. Sha'rāwī warned against judging the truthfulness of the Qur'ān by comparing it to scientific developments, for the Qur'ān should always be epistemologically privileged above everything else.

For Further Reflection

1. John Hedley Brooke outlines three positions, each of which tends to overstate the relationship between science and religion. The first, the

conflict model, holds the effects of science and religion to be antagonistic; the second, the separation model, holds that each operates in different realms; the third position is the model of mutual relevance.[12] It is clear that Muḥammad ʿAbduh and the Commission on Scientific Signs of Qurʾān and Sunnah take the third position. But where do the approaches of al-Shaʿrāwī and Quṭb belong in such a scheme?

2. If we agree that holy scripture can only ever be accessed by humans through their own human (fallible) interpretations and conditioned by their particular social and historical contexts, then how does this complicate Quṭb's and Shaʿrāwī's assertions of the distinction between imperfect human science and perfect divine scripture?

3. The opposition of society and nature has been the main object of critique by contemporary philosophers and sociologists of science. Most notably, Bruno Latour, in his important book *We Have Never Been Modern*, argues that society and nature have always been intertwined, and our insistence on seeing them as separate has led to theoretical and practical mistakes of catastrophic proportion (such as global warming and microbial resistance to antibiotics). Latour, who advocates a sort of pantheism and refuses to discuss divine agency, proposes that the social and natural worlds are necessarily intertwined.[13]

4. Does the bifurcation of the human and divine correspond to the post-Enlightenment European bifurcation of society and nature? Does the human realm reflect the social; the divine realm, the natural? Some Muslim thinkers, such as Seyyed Hossein Nasr, argue that, because of the Islamic principle of *tawḥīd*, Islam does not know this opposition; God transcends this division because humans can only act and create within the divine will.

5. Both Quṭb and Shaʿrāwī, in Ashʿari fashion, regard the tension between God's will and human agency as beyond the comprehension of humans, knowledge that exists with God alone. Does this contradict their other claim that human knowledge and divine knowledge are utterly distinct realms? Is the dichotomous conception of society against nature, as Bruno Latour suggests, a product of modernity? How would ʿAbduh's insistence on reason and rationality in faith reconcile this?

6. Further, it would seem that the bifurcation of the human and divine realms, as upheld by both Quṭb and Shaʿrāwī, is transgressed by devout

believers who are also scientists. For Quṭb, if all human knowledge is necessarily imperfect and only God has perfect knowledge, is there a way for humans to assess which claims to knowledge are more or less true than others?

Notes

1. Sayyid Quṭb, *In the Shade of the Qur'ān*, vol. 1 (Leicester: Islamic Foundation, 1999), 200.

2. Muḥammad 'Abduh, *al-Islām wa-'l-naṣrāniyya ma'a al-'ilm wa-'l-madaniyya* (Cairo: Maṭba'at al-Manār, 1905), 171–72.

3. Ahmed Bouzid, *Man, Society, and Knowledge in the Islamist Discourse of Sayyid Quṭb* (Ph.D. diss., Virginia Polytechnic Institute, 1998), 43.

4. Ibid., 41–42.

5. Jakob Skovgaard-Petersen, *Defining Islam for the Egyptian State* (Leiden: Brill, 1996), 12.

6. These fatwas/*responsa* are found in the compilation *Muḥammad Mutwallī al-Sha'rāwī: al-Fatāwā al-ḳubrā*, 2nd ed. (Cairo: Maktabat al-Turāth al-Islāmī, 2002).

7. The title of my book *Our Bodies Belong to God* is a quotation from Shaykh al-Sha'rāwī (Sherine Hamdy, *Our Bodies Belong to God: Organ Transplants, Islam, and the Struggle for Human Dignity in Egypt* [Berkeley: University of California Press, 2012]). Inadvertently finding himself at the center of a national debate in Egypt about science and medicine, he provocatively asked, "How could you give away a kidney that you yourself do not own?" This question reflects his stance toward medical intervention in end-of-life care as well as his aversion toward the idea of organ transplantation.

8. Shaykh Muḥammad Mitwallī al-Sha'rāwī, *The Miracles of the Qur'ān* (London: Dar al-Taqwa, 1989), 65.

9. The point about modern embryology is also made by a scientist from the French Academy of Medicine, Maurice Bucaille. He defends his conviction that the Qur'ān was revealed to a prophet on the basis of its verses referring to embryonic development, arguing that it was unthinkable for a man of Muḥammad's time to have been the author of such statements, given the state of knowledge in his day. In a work first published in 1976, and well known throughout the Muslim world, Bucaille writes: "I knew from translations that the Qur'an often made allusion to all sorts of natural phenomena, but I only had a summary knowledge. It was only when I examined the text very closely in Arabic that . . . I had to acknowledge the evidence in front of me: the Qur'an did not contain a single statement that was assailable from a modern scientific point of view" (Maurice Bucaille, *The Bible, the Qur'an, and Science: The Holy Scriptures Examined in the Light of Modern Knowledge* [Elmhurst, NY: Tahrike Tarsile Qur'an, 2003], 19). Because excerpts from Bucaille's lectures and writings were widely distributed by Saudi Arabia in the 1970s, the notion that modern embryology was anticipated in the Qur'ān gained the status of a self-evident truth claim.

10. For the website, see www.eajaz.org/eajaz/index.php?lang=en.

11. Marwa Elshakry, "The Exegesis of Science in Twentieth Century Arabic Interpretations of the Qur'an," in *Nature and Scripture in the Abrahamic Religions: 1700–Present*, vol. 1, Jitse M. van der Meer and Scott Mandelbrote, eds. (Leiden: Brill, 2008), 521.

12. John Hedley Brooke, *Science and Religion: Some Historical Perspectives* (Cambridge: Cambridge University Press, 1991), 2–4.

13. Bruno Latour, *We Have Never Been Modern* (Cambridge, MA: Harvard University Press, 1993).

Pope John Paul II

Letter of his Holiness John Paul II to the Reverend George V. Coyne, SJ, Director of the Vatican Observatory

To the Reverend George V. Coyne, SJ, Director of the Vatican Observatory

"Grace to you and peace from God our Father and the Lord Jesus Christ" (Eph 1:2).

As you prepare to publish the papers presented at the Study Week held at Castel Gandolfo on 21–26 September 1987, I take the occasion to express my gratitude to you and through you to all who contributed to that important initiative. I am confident that the publication of these papers will ensure that the fruits of that endeavour will be further enriched.

The three hundredth anniversary of the publication of Newton's *Philosophiae Naturalis Principia Mathematica* provided an appropriate occasion for the Holy See to sponsor a Study Week that investigated the multiple relationships among theology, philosophy and the natural sciences. The man so honoured, Sir Isaac Newton, had himself devoted much of his life to these same issues, and his reflections upon them can be found throughout his major works, his unfinished manuscripts and his vast correspondence. The publication of your own papers from this Study Week, taking up again some of the same questions which this great genius explored, affords me the opportunity to thank you for the efforts you devoted to a subject of such paramount importance. The theme of your conference, "Our Knowledge of God and Nature: Physics, Philosophy and Theology," is assuredly a crucial one for the contemporary world. Because of its importance, I should like to address some issues which the interactions among natural science, philosophy, and theology present to the Church and to human society in general.

The Church and the Academy engage one another as two very different but major institutions within human civilization and world culture. We bear before God enormous responsibilities for the human condition because histori-cally we have had and continue to have a major influence on the development of ideas and values and on the course of human action. We both have histories stretching back over thousands of years: the learned, academic community dating back to the origins of culture, to the city and the library and the school, and the Church with her historical roots in ancient Israel. We have come into contact often during these centuries, sometimes in mutual support, at other times in those needless conflicts which have marred both our histories. In your conference we met again, and it was altogether fitting that as we approach the close of this millennium we initiated a series of reflections together upon the world as we touch it and as it shapes and challenges our actions.

So much of our world seems to be in fragments, in disjointed pieces. So much of human life is passed in isolation or in hostility. The division between rich nations and poor nations continues to grow; the contrast between north-ern and southern regions of our planet becomes ever more marked and intoler-able. The antagonism between races and religions splits countries into warring camps; historical animosities show no signs of abating. Even within the aca-demic community, the separation between truth and values persists, and the isolation of their several cultures—scientific, humanistic and religious—makes common discourse difficult if not at times impossible.

But at the same time we see in large sectors of the human community a growing critical openness towards people of different cultures and back-grounds, different competencies and viewpoints. More and more frequently, people are seeking intellectual coherence and collaboration, and are discover-ing values and experiences they have in common even within their diversities. This openness, this dynamic interchange, is a notable feature of the interna-tional scientific communities themselves, and is based on common interests, common goals and a common enterprise, along with a deep awareness that the insights and attainments of one are often important for the progress of the other. In a similar but more subtle way this has occurred and is continuing to occur among more diverse group—among the communities that make up the Church, and even between the scientific community and the Church herself. This drive is essentially a movement towards the kind of unity which resists homogenization and relishes diversity. Such community is determined by a common meaning and by a shared understanding that evokes a sense of mutual involvement. Two groups which may seem initially to have nothing in common can begin to enter into community with one another by discovering a common goal, and this in turn can lead to broader areas of shared understanding and concern.

As never before in her history, the Church has entered into the movement for the union of all Christians, fostering common study, prayer, and discussions that "all may be one" (Io 17:20). She has attempted to rid herself of every vestige of antisemitism and to emphasize her origins in and her religious debt to Judaism. In reflection and prayer, she has reached out to the great world religions, recognizing the values we all hold in common and our universal and utter dependence upon God.

Within the Church herself, there is a growing sense of "world church," so much in evidence at the last Ecumenical Council in which bishops native to every continent—no longer predominantly of European or even Western origin—assumed for the first time their common responsibility for the entire Church. The documents from that Council and of the magisterium have reflected this new world-consciousness both in their content and in their attempt to address all people of good will. During this century, we have witnessed a dynamic tendency to reconciliation and unity that has taken many forms within the Church.

Nor should such a development be surprising. The Christian community in moving so emphatically in this direction is realizing in greater intensity the activity of Christ within her: "For God was in Christ, reconciling the world to himself" (2 Cor 5:19). We ourselves are called to be a continuation of the reconciliation of human beings, one with another and all with God. Our very nature as Church entails this commitment to unity.

Turning to the relationship between religion and science, there has been a definite, though still fragile and provisional, movement towards a new and more nuanced interchange. We have begun to talk to one another on deeper levels than before, and with greater openness towards one another's perspectives. We have begun to search together for a more thorough understanding of one another's disciplines, with their competencies and their limitations, and especially for areas of common ground. In doing so we have uncovered important questions which concern both of us, and which are vital to the larger human community we both serve. It is crucial that this common search based on critical openness and interchange should not only continue but also grow and deepen in its quality and scope.

For the impact each has, and will continue to have, on the course of civilization and on the world itself, cannot be overestimated, and there is so much that each can offer the other. There is, of course, the vision of the unity of all things and all peoples in Christ, who is active and present with us in our daily lives—in our struggles, our sufferings, our joys and in our searchings—and who is the focus of the Church's life and witness. This vision carries with it into the larger community a deep reverence for all that is, a hope and assurance that the fragile goodness, beauty and life we see in the universe is moving towards a completion and fulfilment which will not be overwhelmed by the forces of dissolution and death. This vision also provides a strong support for the values which are emerging both from our knowledge and appreciation of creation and of ourselves as the products, knowers and stewards of creation.

The scientific disciplines too, as is obvious, are endowing us with an understanding and appreciation of our universe as a whole and of the incredibly rich variety of intricately related processes and structures which constitute its animate and inanimate components. This knowledge has given us a more thorough understanding of ourselves and of our humble yet unique role within creation. Through technology it also has given us the capacity to travel, to communicate, to build, to cure, and to probe in ways which would have been almost unimaginable to our ancestors. Such knowledge and power, as we have discovered, can be used greatly to enhance and improve our lives or they can be exploited to diminish and destroy human life and the environment even on a global scale.

The unity we perceive in creation on the basis of our faith in Jesus Christ as Lord of the universe, and the correlative unity for which we strive in our human communities, seems to be reflected and even reinforced in what contemporary science is revealing to us. As we behold the incredible development of scientific research we detect an underlying movement towards the discovery of levels of law and process which unify created reality and which at the same time have given rise to the vast diversity of structures and organisms which constitute the physical and biological, and even the psychological and sociological, worlds.

Contemporary physics furnishes a striking example. The quest for the unification of all four fundamental physical forces—gravitation, electromagnetism, the strong and weak nuclear interactions—has met with increasing success. This unification may well combine discoveries from the sub-atomic and the cosmological domains and shed light both on the origin of the universe and, eventually, on the origin of the laws and constants which govern its evolution. Physicists possess a detailed though incomplete and provisional knowledge of elementary particles and of the fundamental forces through which they interact at low and intermediate energies. They now have an acceptable theory unifying the electro-magnetic and weak nuclear forces, along with much less adequate but still promising grand unified field theories which attempt to incorporate the strong nuclear interaction as well. Further in the line of this same development, there are already several detailed suggestions for the final stage, superunification, that is, the unification of all four fundamental forces, including gravity. Is it not important for us to note that in a world of such detailed specialization as contemporary physics there exists this drive towards convergence?

In the life sciences, too, something similar has happened. Molecular biologists have probed the structure of living material, its functions and its processes of replication. They have discovered that the same underlying constituents serve in the make-up of all living organisms on earth and constitute both the genes and the proteins which these genes code. This is another impressive manifestation of the unity of nature.

By encouraging openness between the Church and the scientific communities, we are not envisioning a disciplinary unity between theology and science like that which exists within a given scientific field or within theology proper. As dialogue and common searching continue, there will be growth towards mutual understanding and a gradual uncovering of common concerns which will provide the basis for further research and discussion. Exactly what form that will take must be left to the future. What is important, as we have already stressed, is that the dialogue should continue and grow in depth and scope. In the process we must overcome every regressive tendency to a unilateral reductionism, to fear, and to self-imposed isolation. What is critically important is that each discipline should continue to enrich, nourish and challenge the other to be more fully what it can be and to contribute to our vision of who we are and who we are becoming.

We might ask whether or not we are ready for this crucial endeavour. Is the community of world religions, including the Church, ready to enter into a more thorough-going dialogue with the scientific community, a dialogue in which the integrity of both religion and science is supported and the advance of each is fostered? Is the scientific community now prepared to open itself to Christianity, and indeed to all the great world religions, working with us all to build a culture that is more humane and in that way more divine? Do we dare to risk the honesty and the courage that this task demands? We must ask ourselves whether both science and religion will contribute to the integration of human culture or to its fragmentation. It is a single choice and it confronts us all.

For a simple neutrality is no longer acceptable. If they are to grow and mature, peoples cannot continue to live in separate compartments, pursuing totally divergent interests from which they evaluate and judge their world. A divided community fosters a fragmented vision of the world; a community of interchange encourages its members to expand their partial perspectives and form a new unified vision.

Yet the unity that we seek, as we have already stressed, is not identity. The Church does not propose that science should become religion or religion science. On the contrary, unity always presupposes the diversity and the integrity of its elements. Each of these members should become not less itself but more itself in a dynamic interchange, for a unity in which one of the elements is reduced to the other is destructive, false in its promises of harmony, and ruinous of the integrity of its components. We are asked to become one. We are not asked to become each other.

To be more specific, both religion and science must preserve their autonomy and their distinctiveness. Religion is not founded on science nor is science an extension of religion. Each should possess its own principles, its pattern of procedures, its diversities of interpretation and its own conclusions. Christianity possesses the source of its justification within itself and does not expect science to constitute its primary apologetic. Science must bear witness to its own worth. While each can and should support the other as distinct dimensions of a common human culture, neither ought to assume that it forms a necessary premise for the other. The unprecedented opportunity we have today is for a common interactive relationship in which each discipline retains its integrity and yet is radically open to the discoveries and insights of the other.

But why is critical openness and mutual interchange a value for both of us? Unity involves the drive of the human mind towards understanding and the desire of the human spirit for love. When human beings seek to understand the multiplicities that surround them, when they seek to make sense of experience, they do so by bringing many factors into a common vision. Understanding is achieved when many data are unified by a common structure. The one illuminates the many: it makes sense of the whole. Simple multiplicity is chaos; an insight, a single model, can give that chaos structure and draw it into intelligibility. We move towards unity as we move towards meaning in our lives. Unity is also the consequence of love. If love is genuine, it moves not towards the assimilation of the other but towards union with the other. Human community begins in desire when that union has not been achieved, and it is completed in joy when those who have been apart are now united.

In the Church's earliest documents, the realization of community, in the radical sense of that word, was seen as the promise and goal of the Gospel: "That which we have seen and heard we proclaim also to you, so that you may have fellowship with us; and our fellowship is with the Father and with his Son Jesus Christ. And we are writing this that our joy may be complete" (1 Io 1:3–4). Later the Church reached out to the sciences and to the arts, founding great universities and building monuments of surpassing beauty so that all things might be recapitulated in Christ (cf. Eph 1:10).

What, then, does the Church encourage in this relational unity between science and religion? First and foremost that they should come to understand one another. For too long a time they have been at arm's length. Theology has been defined as an effort of faith to achieve understanding, as *fides quaerens intellectum*. As such, it must be in vital interchange today with science just as it always has been with philosophy and other forms of learning. Theology will have to call on the findings of science to one degree or another as it pursues its primary concern for the human person, the reaches of freedom, the possibilities of Christian community, the nature of belief and the intelligibility of nature and history. The vitality and significance of theology for humanity will in a profound way be reflected in its ability to incorporate these findings.

Now this is a point of delicate importance, and it has to be carefully qualified. Theology is not to incorporate indifferently each new philosophical or scientific theory. As these findings become part of the intellectual culture of the time, however, theologians must understand them and test their value in bringing out from Christian belief some of the possibilities which have not yet been realized. The hylomorphism of Aristotelian natural philosophy, for example, was adopted by the medieval theologians to help them explore the nature of the sacraments and the hypostatic union. This did not mean that the Church adjudicated the truth or falsity of the Aristotelian insight, since that is not her concern. It did mean that this was one of the rich insights offered by Greek culture, that it needed to be understood and taken seriously and tested for its value in illuminating various areas of theology. Theologians might well ask, with respect to contemporary science, philosophy and the other areas of human knowing, if they have accomplished this extraordinarily difficult process as well as did these medieval masters.

If the cosmologies of the ancient Near Eastern world could be purified and assimilated into the first chapters of Genesis, might not contemporary cosmology have something to offer to our reflections upon creation? Does an evolutionary perspective bring any light to bear upon theological anthropology, the meaning of the human person as the *imago Dei*, the problem of Christology—and even upon the development of doctrine itself? What, if any, are the eschatological implications of contemporary cosmology, especially in light of the vast future of our universe? Can theological method fruitfully appropriate insights from scientific methodology and the philosophy of science?

Questions of this kind can be suggested in abundance. Pursuing them further would require the sort of intense dialogue with contemporary science that has, on the whole, been lacking among those engaged in theological research and teaching. It would entail that some theologians, at least, should be sufficiently well versed in the sciences to make authentic and creative use of the resources that the best-established theories may offer them. Such an expertise would prevent them from making uncritical and overhasty use for apologetic purposes of such recent theories as that of the "Big Bang" in cosmology. Yet it would equally keep them from discounting altogether the potential relevance of such theories to the deepening of understanding in traditional areas of theological inquiry.

In this process of mutual learning, those members of the Church who are themselves either active scientists or, in some special cases, both scientists and theologians could serve as a key resource. They can also provide a much-needed ministry to others struggling to integrate the worlds of science and religion in their own intellectual and spiritual lives, as well as to those who face difficult moral decisions in matters of technological research and application. Such bridging ministries must be nurtured and encouraged. The Church long ago recognized the importance of such links by establishing the Pontifical

Academy of Sciences, in which some of the world's leading scientists meet together regularly to discuss their researches and to convey to the larger community where the directions of discovery are tending. But much more is needed.

The matter is urgent. Contemporary developments in science challenge theology far more deeply than did the introduction of Aristotle into Western Europe in the thirteenth century. Yet these developments also offer to theology a potentially important resource. Just as Aristotelian philosophy, through the ministry of such great scholars as St. Thomas Aquinas, ultimately came to shape some of the most profound expressions of theological doctrine, so can we not hope that the sciences of today, along with all forms of human knowing, may invigorate and inform those parts of the theological enterprise that bear on the relation of nature, humanity and God?

Can science also benefit from this interchange? It would seem that it should. For science develops best when its concepts and conclusions are integrated into the broader human culture and its concerns for ultimate meaning and value. Scientists cannot, therefore, hold themselves entirely aloof from the sorts of issues dealt with by philosophers and theologians. By devoting to these issues something of the energy and care they give to their research in science, they can help others realize more fully the human potentialities of their discoveries. They can also come to appreciate for themselves that these discoveries cannot be a genuine substitute for knowledge of the truly ultimate. Science can purify religion from error and superstition; religion can purify science from idolatry and false absolutes. Each can draw the other into a wider world, a world in which both can flourish.

For the truth of the matter is that the Church and the scientific community will inevitably interact; their options do not include isolation. Christians will inevitably assimilate the prevailing ideas about the world, and today these are deeply shaped by science. The only question is whether they will do this critically or unreflectively, with depth and nuance or with a shallowness that debases the Gospel and leaves us ashamed before history. Scientists, like all human beings, will make decisions upon what ultimately gives meaning and value to their lives and to their work. This they will do well or poorly, with the reflective depth that theological wisdom can help them attain, or with an unconsidered absolutizing of their results beyond their reasonable and proper limits.

Both the Church and the scientific community are faced with such inescapable alternatives. We shall make our choices much better if we live in a collaborative interaction in which we are called continually to be more. Only a dynamic relationship between theology and science can reveal those limits which support the integrity of either discipline, so that theology does not profess a pseudo-science and science does not become an unconscious theology. Our knowledge of each other can lead us to be more authentically ourselves. No one can read the history of the past century and not realize that crisis is upon us both. The uses of science have on more than one occasion proved massively destructive, and the reflections on religion have too often been sterile. We need each other to be what we must be, what we are called to be.

And so on this occasion of the Newton Tercentennial, the Church speaking through my ministry calls upon herself and the scientific community to intensify their constructive relations of interchange through unity. You are called to learn from one another, to renew the context in which science is done and to nourish the inculturation which vital theology demands. Each of you has everything to gain from such an interaction, and the human community which we both serve has a right to demand it from us.

Upon all who participated in the Study Week sponsored by the Holy See and upon all who will read and study the papers herein published I invoke wisdom and peace in our Lord Jesus Christ and cordially impart my Apostolic Blessing.

From the Vatican, 1 June 1988.[1]

Address of Pope John Paul II to the Pontifical Academy of Sciences (October 22, 1996)

With great pleasure I address cordial greeting to you, Mr. President, and to all of you who constitute the Pontifical Academy of Sciences, on the occasion of your plenary assembly. I offer my best wishes in particular to the new academicians, who have come to take part in your work for the first time. I would also like to remember the academicians who died during the past year, whom I commend to the Lord of life.

1. In celebrating the 60th anniversary of the academy's refoundation, I would like to recall the intentions of my predecessor Pius XI, who wished to surround himself with a select group of scholars, relying on them to inform the Holy See in complete freedom about developments in scientific research, and thereby to assist him in his reflections.

He asked those whom he called the Church's "senatus scientificus" to serve the truth. I again extend this same invitation to you today, certain that we will be able to profit from the fruitfulness of a trustful dialogue between the Church and science (cf. Address to the Academy of Sciences, No. 1, Oct. 28, 1986; *L'Osservatore Romano, Eng. ed.*, Nov. 24, 1986, p. 22).

2. I am pleased with the first theme you have chosen, that of the origins of life and evolution, an essential subject which deeply interests the Church, since revelation, for its part, contains teaching concerning the nature and origins of man. How do the conclusions reached by the various scientific disciplines coincide with those contained in the message of revelation? And if, at first sight, there are apparent contradictions, in what direction do we look for their solution? We know, in fact, that truth cannot contradict truth (cf. Leo XIII, encyclical *Providentissimus Deus*). Moreover, to shed greater light on historical truth, your research on the Church's relations with science between the 16th and 18th centuries is of great importance. During this plenary session, you are undertaking a "reflection on science at the dawn of the third millennium," starting with the identification of the principal problems created by the sciences and which affect humanity's future. With this step you point the way to solutions which will be beneficial to the whole human community. In the domain of inanimate and animate nature, the evolution of science and its applications give rise to new questions. The better the Church's knowledge is of their essential aspects, the more she will understand their impact. Consequently, in accordance with her specific mission she will be able to offer criteria for discerning the moral conduct required of all human beings in view of their integral salvation.

3. Before offering you several reflections that more specifically concern the subject of the origin of life and its evolution, I would like to remind you that the magisterium of the Church has already made pronouncements on these

matters within the framework of her own competence. I will cite here two interventions.

In his encyclical *Humani Generis* (1950), my predecessor Pius XII had already stated that there was no opposition between evolution and the doctrine of the faith about man and his vocation, on condition that one did not lose sight of several indisputable points.

For my part, when I received those taking part in your academy's plenary assembly on October 31, 1992, I had the opportunity with regard to Galileo to draw attention to the need of a rigorous hermeneutic for the correct interpretation of the inspired word. It is necessary to determine the proper sense of Scripture, while avoiding any unwarranted interpretations that make it say what it does not intend to say. In order to delineate the field of their own study, the exegete and the theologian must keep informed about the results achieved by the natural sciences (cf. AAS 85 1/81993 3/8, pp. 764–772; address to the Pontifical Biblical Commission, April 23, 1993, announcing the document on the *The Interpretation of the Bible in the Church*: AAS 86 1/81994 3/8, pp. 232–243).

4. Taking into account the state of scientific research at the time as well as of the requirements of theology, the encyclical *Humani Generis* considered the doctrine of "evolutionism" a serious hypothesis, worthy of investigation and in-depth study equal to that of the opposing hypothesis. Pius XII added two methodological conditions: that this opinion should not be adopted as though it were a certain, proven doctrine and as though one could totally prescind from revelation with regard to the questions it raises. He also spelled out the condition on which this opinion would be compatible with the Christian faith, a point to which I will return. Today, almost half a century after the publication of the encyclical, new knowledge has led to the recognition of the theory of evolution as more than a hypothesis. [Aujourdhui, près d'un demi-siècle après la parution de l'encyclique, de nouvelles connaissances conduisent à reconnaitre dans la théorie de l'évolution plus qu'une hypothèse.] It is indeed remarkable that this theory has been progressively accepted by researchers, following a series of discoveries in various fields of knowledge. The convergence, neither sought nor fabricated, of the results of work that was conducted independently is in itself a significant argument in favor of this theory.

What is the significance of such a theory? To address this question is to enter the field of epistemology. A theory is a metascientific elaboration, distinct from the results of observation but consistent with them. By means of it a series of independent data and facts can be related and interpreted in a unified explanation. A theory's validity depends on whether or not it can be verified; it is constantly tested against the facts; wherever it can no longer explain the latter, it shows its limitations and unsuitability. It must then be rethought.

Furthermore, while the formulation of a theory like that of evolution complies with the need for consistency with the observed data, it borrows certain notions from natural philosophy.

And, to tell the truth, rather than the theory of evolution, we should speak of several theories of evolution. On the one hand, this plurality has to do with the different explanations advanced for the mechanism of evolution, and on the other, with the various philosophies on which it is based. Hence the existence of materialist, reductionist and spiritualist interpretations. What is to be decided here is the true role of philosophy and, beyond it, of theology.

5. The Church's magisterium is directly concerned with the question of evolution, for it involves the conception of man: Revelation teaches us that he was created in the image and likeness of God (cf. Gen 1:27–29). The conciliar constitution *Gaudium et Spes* has magnificently explained this doctrine, which is pivotal to Christian thought. It recalled that man is "the only creature on earth that God has wanted for its own sake" (No. 24). In other terms, the human individual cannot be subordinated as a pure means or a pure instrument, either to the species or to society; he has value *per se*. He is a person. With his intellect and his will, he is capable of forming a relationship of communion, solidarity and self-giving with his peers. St. Thomas observes that man's likeness to God resides especially in his speculative intellect, for his relationship with the object of his knowledge resembles God's relationship with what he has created (*Summa Theologica* I–II:3:5, ad 1). But even more, man is called to enter into a relationship of knowledge and love with God himself, a relationship which will find its complete fulfillment beyond time, in eternity. All the depth and grandeur of this vocation are revealed to us in the mystery of the risen Christ (cf. *Gaudium et Spes*, 22). It is by virtue of his spiritual soul that the whole person possesses such a dignity even in his body. Pius XII stressed this essential point: If the human body take its origin from

pre-existent living matter, the spiritual soul is immediately created by God ("animas enim a Deo immediate creari catholica fides nos retinere iubei"; "Humani Generis," 36). Consequently, theories of evolution which, in accordance with the philosophies inspiring them, consider the spirit as emerging from the forces of living matter or as a mere *epiphenomenon* of this matter, are incompatible with the truth about man. Nor are they able to ground the dignity of the person.

6. With man, then, we find ourselves in the presence of an ontological difference, an ontological leap, one could say. However, does not the posing of such ontological discontinuity run counter to that physical continuity which seems to be the main thread of research into evolution in the field of physics and chemistry? Consideration of the method used in the various branches of knowledge makes it possible to reconcile two points of view which would seem irreconcilable. The sciences of observation describe and measure the multiple manifestations of life with increasing precision and correlate them with the time line. The moment of transition to the spiritual cannot be the object of this kind of observation, which nevertheless can discover at the experimental level a series of very valuable signs indicating what is specific to the human being. But the experience of metaphysical knowledge, of self-awareness and self-reflection, of moral conscience, freedom, or again of aesthetic and religious experience, falls within the competence of philosophical analysis and reflection, while theology brings out its ultimate meaning according to the Creator's plans.

7. In conclusion, I would like to call to mind a Gospel truth which can shed a higher light on the horizon of your research into the origins and unfolding of living matter. The Bible in fact bears an extraordinary message of life. It gives us a wise vision of life inasmuch as it describes the loftiest forms of existence. This vision guided me in the encyclical which I dedicated to respect for human life, and which I called precisely "Evangelium Vitae."

It is significant that in St. John's Gospel *life* refers to the divine light which Christ communicates to us. We are called to enter into eternal life, that is to say, into the eternity of divine beatitude. To warn us against the serious temptations threatening us, our Lord quotes the great saying of Deuteronomy: "Man shall not live by bread alone, but by every word that proceeds from the mouth of God" (Dt 8:3; cf. Mt 4:4). Even more, "life" is one of the most beautiful titles which the Bible attributes to God. He is the living God.

I cordially invoke an abundance of divine blessings upon you and upon all who are close to you.[2]

Notes

1. Libreria Editrice Vaticana, accessed September 8, 2011, www.vatican.va/holy_father/ john_paul_ii/letters/1988/documents/hf_jp-i i_let_19880601_padre-coyne_en.html.

2. Libreria Editrice Vaticana, excerpted from *L'Osservatore Romano* (English edition), October 30, 1996. Available at NewAdvent.org, accessed September 8, 2011, www.newadvent.org/ library/docs_jp02tc.htm.

Commentary

CELIA DEANE-DRUMMOND

THE TONE OF Pope John Paul II's 1988 letter to Fr. George Coyne is conciliatory, rather than hostile, toward science, especially scientific research. This is important because it counteracts and qualifies some of his other statements that are mostly directed toward those areas of science, such as particular branches of medicine, that have more direct ethical implications for Catholics. The recognition that many of the past conflicts between the Roman Catholic Church and the scientific Academy were "needless" does not exactly amount to an apology but comes close to it. Such conflicts, however, are also situated more widely within the divisions within society at a religious, national, or global level.

John Paul II's desire now is for "common discourse" between the sciences and among disparate religions but without covering over differences: in this respect he desires a celebration of diversity rather than homogenization. This is, I believe, extremely important for collaborative ventures such as this seminar, for diversity needs to be allowed to flourish, but in such a way that unity and reconciliation rather than conflict emerge. At the same time, more specifically within the science and religion discourse, he is open to the possibility of finding genuine common ground as well as the insights that come through viewing the same issue from a completely different perspective.

This basic stance of openness to the insights of modern science flows most naturally from a wider appreciation within the Roman Catholic tradition of the value of reason as such. The opening remarks of the 1998 encyclical *Fides et ratio* make clear that faith and reason are "like two wings on which the human spirit rises to the contemplation of the truth."[1] Yet even more significant, perhaps, is the insight that truth is grounded in an encounter with wisdom as found in scriptural texts, such as Proverbs or the Book of Wisdom (§16–19). This sets the stage for the relationship between reason and faith, for in the light of wisdom "reason is valued without being overvalued" (§20). The search goes on, therefore, not in the name of the acquisition of knowledge for its own sake, but for the sake of searching for the truth, understood according to the classical notion of that which is beautiful, good, and true (§21). Science is therefore treated in a similar manner to other secular philosophies that are subject to distortions because of the sinful human condition arising out of the "primal disobedience" as told in the book of Genesis (§22). The possibility that there might be a clash between the wisdom found in the world and that articulated through faith in Christ allows for a critical approach to science in the light of faith traditions. In particular, drawing on the first letter of Paul to the Corinthians, the emphasis on the contrast between the wisdom of this world and the wisdom of God revealed in the foolishness of the cross of Christ means that there can be no premature claim to possess the truth (§23). The conclusion of this encyclical includes the following statement that clarifies how science should be conducted from this perspective: "In expressing my admiration and in offering encouragement to these brave pioneers of scientific research, to whom humanity owes much of its current development, I would urge them to continue their efforts without abandoning the *sapiential* horizon within which scientific and technological achievements are wedded to the philosophical and ethical values which are the distinctive mark of the human person" (§106).

Embedded in the letter to Coyne we find expressions of John Paul II's commitment to traditional affirmations of God as Creator, of the natural world as gift, and of humans as those responsible for appropriate care of creation, or stewardship. The letter also conveys a theme that he raises repeatedly in other documents, namely, his overriding sense of the world's fragile environmental state, pressed by the continuing demands of a consumer society, particularly among richer nations.[2] This is one area, at least, where scientific and religious values can cooperate in facing such global social and environmental challenges. The environmental themes peppered throughout Pope John Paul II's work come to fruition in the way that Pope Benedict XVI has subsequently expressed the tasks for human society as a whole in his 2009 encyclical on social teaching, *Caritas in veritate*.[3] A common thread here is a deep valuation of the human person, so that even if environmental concerns are near to the fore, this indicates not so much a turn to nature as a recognition of the ecological and social networks in which human life is placed. John

Paul II adopted the phrase "human ecology" to describe this close connection between human and ecological concerns. He can conclude that "not only is a 'physical' ecology at stake, attentive to safeguarding the habitat of different living beings, but also a 'human' ecology that will render the life of creatures more dignified, protecting the radical good of life in all its manifestations and preparing an environment for future generations that is closer to the plan of the Creator."[4]

In the letter to Coyne we also find acknowledgment that particular physical and biological processes have given rise to the diversity of life around us and, perhaps even more remarkably, an admission that this also applies to "the psychological and sociological worlds." John Paul II turns to physics to note the drive toward a theory that seeks to explain all fundamental forces (gravitation, electromagnetism, and strong and weak nuclear forces) in terms of one unified theory. In biology, too, the discovery of a common genetic code is testimony to the unity within the natural world. Yet he notes that such a development in the sciences is also culturally situated, that is, it finds common ground with a shift toward mutual understanding that is detectable in contemporary societies. It is this mutual respect that he wishes to highlight so that common concerns will inform dialogue and discussion. In the context of this seminar, the common ground sought is more complex and multifarious because it is not just that between science and a religious tradition but across religious traditions. John Paul II's call that each tradition should "enrich, nourish and challenge the other" is a vision worth pursuing. But he is also aware of the difficulties of such a task. Are we ready now, over twenty years on? Will science and religion indeed contribute to the integration of human culture or its fragmentation? John Paul II's concern that each should become more fully itself shows his respect for different cultures and traditions. How far either the Church or the scientific community have pursued such a vision in practice may be debatable, but this is not the issue to contend with here.

In terms of the science and religion discourse, John Paul II presses for mutual exchange and interchange rather than synthesis. This is sensible at a theoretical level, but is it achievable in practice? The temptation toward synthesis may be just as damaging as that toward fragmentation. These are, perhaps, the difficulties faced by those engaged in the dialogue between different religious traditions. The Christian tradition has, I believe, suffered from a surfeit of synthetic maneuvers, partly in reaction to the history of Luddite actions by the Roman Catholic Church that in the past seemed to inhibit the freedoms of scientific discovery and innovation. On the other hand, because of its methodological presuppositions the scientific community has found it hard to be genuinely open to the possibility of insights from religious traditions or to accept that those religious traditions would be preferred over scientific reasoning where the two are in conflict. The genuine love that John Paul II speaks of as a necessary prerequisite for such forms of dialogue is hard to come by but not necessarily impossible.

It is certainly bold to call for a genuine drawing by theology on scientific research, to the same extent that theology draws on philosophy, for such an attitude to scientific research is rarely found within the academic theological community. Yet John Paul II also remains cautious as to how this might be done, for he treats scientific knowledge as that which enables insights from Christian traditions to become fully appreciated. But does this really reflect learning, or does it amount to a rationalization of prior concepts? For the scientific community, the awareness of broader human values is becoming increasingly recognized, but is there anything specifically religious here, or could such a challenge come equally from philosophies such as humanism? In the language of wisdom we can see both what the Christian tradition shares with other traditions and what is distinctive about it. Here, as discussed earlier, the cross of Christ challenges too great adherence to alternative ways of thinking and acting. Yet it takes considerable powers of discernment to distinguish between those cases where the cross is appropriately brought into play when there are difficulties in relation to scientific knowledge, and those places where it might be used as a means of promoting a particular position that is not necessarily self-evident. The keenest difficulties are found in the exploration of bioethical issues, where the approach of the official magisterium to the status of the human embryo remains absolute in its conservatism. In this case, genuine theological disagreement among theologians as to what might be permissible according to Christian tradition is sometimes viewed with suspicion under the negative label of "dissent." Part of the difficulty here is the identity of Roman Catholics who, on the one hand, affirm the value of conscience and discernment through obedience to the call of God understood as inspired by the Holy Spirit and, on the other hand, affirm the importance of due submission to ecclesial authority. While technically the only statements that cannot

be altered or challenged by the laity are those rare ones made by papal authority *ex cathedra*, in practice other recommendations become added on to those
requirements, leading to understandable confusion.

The specific treatment of evolutionary theory in the 1996 Address of John
Paul II to the Pontifical Academy of the Sciences, nearly a decade later than
his letter to Fr. Coyne, speaks of the way this theory in particular has gradually
become accommodated within the teaching of the Roman Catholic Church.
He recognizes that biblical literalism is not tenable, instead holding that it is
"necessary to determine the proper sense of Scripture," apparently an indirect
attack on creationism. He seems resistant to "evolutionism," if by that we
mean a metaphysical theory about knowledge that goes beyond scientific
knowledge, even if this term was rather unfortunately used by his predecessor
Pius XII. John Paul II also remarks that evolutionary ideas are more than
simply hypothetical; rather evolution, by which he seems to mean evolution by
natural selection, is "more than a hypothesis."[5] Yet he is not wrong to suggest
that evolutionary debates are by no means settled, even if the primary means of
evolution by natural selection is judged in the scientific community as having a
secure status alongside other subsidiary hypotheses such as genetic drift or
punctuated evolution. Perhaps he was somewhat ill advised to speak of these
as alternative theories, as if Darwin could be fundamentally challenged by
alternatives. Yet the extension of evolutionary theory into sociobiology is arguably contested among scientists, even if it has become more sophisticated in
evolutionary psychology.

The crucial sticking point for evolutionary theory in relation to the teaching
of the Roman Catholic Church is and remains its conception of the human as
a person. The Roman Catholic Church's teaching on human uniqueness and
a particular soul given by God still jars with common biological interpretations
of humanity as products of evolution. As far as Pope John Paul II is concerned,
weakening or reducing the "ontological leap" is a denial of the basic human
dignity and the respect for life that he believes is at the heart of the Gospel
message. It is from this basis, too, that Christians are linked with the life of
Christ, and so enter into eternal life. Yet from what might seem a very small
point of contention there flow all kinds of other contested issues between
the Roman Catholic Church and contemporary science, from resistance to
experimentation on embryos to the portrayal of modern medicine as a "culture
of death." The ideal of reconciliation that Pope John Paul II aspired to in his

1988 letter is urgent at this juncture with science, perhaps more than anywhere else.

For Further Reflection

1. Is a relationship of critical openness and mutual exchange between scientific and religious communities a visionary ideal to be pursued or an impossible dream? In other words, is it realistic and how might it be realized?
2. Is the role of science in the dialogue with religion to illumine insights from religious traditions or should it go further than this?
3. What specific contribution can religion make to scientific endeavors, other than more general challenges to their place in the wider culture?
4. What different aspects of the dialogue between science and religion emerge in Pope John Paul II's specific treatment of evolutionary theory in the 1996 address?

Notes

1. Pope John Paul II, *Faith and Reason, Encyclical Letter, Fides et ratio* (London: Catholic Truth Society, 1998), also available on the Vatican website, www.vatican.va. Hereafter cited in the main text.

2. Many of these remarks are in the form of letters, but in June 2002 John Paul II issued a joint statement, signed by himself and Patriarch Bartholomew I of Constantinople, claiming that "If we examine carefully the social and environmental crisis which the world community is facing, we must conclude that we are still betraying the mandate God has given us: to be stewards called to collaborate with God in watching over creation in holiness and wisdom" (cited in C. Deane-Drummond, *Seeds of Hope: Facing the Challenge of Climate Justice* [London: CAFOD, 2009], 152–53).

3. Pope Benedict XVI, *Caritas in veritate* (London: Catholic Truth Society, 2009).

4. Pope John Paul II, "God Made Man Steward of Creation," Address to General Audience, January 17, 2001, §4, http://www.vatican.va/holy_father/john_paul_ii/audiences/2001/documents/hf_jp-ii_aud_20010117_en.html.

5. The English edition first translated the French original as follows: "Today, more than a half-century after the appearance of that encyclical, some new findings lead us to the recognition of more than one hypothesis within the theory of evolution." This was later amended by official authorities to "more than a hypothesis," but the implication of the French original suggests that "more than a mere hypothesis" might be closer to the nuance intended, namely, that the theory of evolution has gone beyond the first stage of scientific method.

Afterword

Rowan Williams

THE DISCUSSIONS AT THE Istanbul Building Bridges seminar showed very clearly how far our respective traditions faced comparable questions in responding to the challenge—real or imagined—of contemporary scientific thinking. One such question might be summarized as having to do with the nature of knowledge itself. A thinker such as al-Ghazālī can observe that the clear demonstrative methods of mathematics and mathematically based disciplines can lead us to conclude that every genuine kind of knowing must fall within the compass of these methods; if something does not obviously do so, it is not really knowledge. He also notes that the believer may be tempted to react against this by taking a negative attitude toward science as such. But Ghazālī affirms that this kind of negativity is an offense against true belief— just as Augustine warns against the danger of making faith ridiculous by using scientifically absurd arguments or failing to be as well-informed as possible about the realities of the world we inhabit. In other words, religious believers can properly say that scientific knowing is valid and essential without assuming that it is the only possible mode in which truth is learned. If it is part of the common heritage of religious metaphysics in Islam and Christianity that creation itself presupposes a coherent system of finite causality (although Ghazālī, for example, is careful to insist that the presupposition of a coherent causality cannot be treated as a *necessity*, and his denial of the need for a clear and comprehensive assumption of uniform causal patterns in finite being proved controversial), then the rational investigation of finite causality cannot be an offense to faith; quite the opposite. The refusal to engage in this looks like a betrayal of faith. Both Islam and Christianity have known theologians and philosophers who have dismissed the need for any knowledge other than that offered in revelation (Tertullian is a prominent Christian example). But the mainstream in both faiths has in effect worked on the assumption that

173

what is revealed about God's relation with the finite order is itself a license to explore that order with consistency and dedication.

If we tease out a little further what is and is not being claimed in the metaphysic that is largely common to Christianity and Islam, it would be something along these lines. The finite world is not a realm of necessity; only God is what he is "necessarily," in the sense that God is subject to no other agency and has no contingent qualities. God does not "happen" to be omnipotent or wise; rather, when you have said "God," you must, to be consistent, mean a life that is all-powerful and all-knowing. Nothing else is what it is by definition; it grows and decays, it is subject to chance. Yet what is not necessary is not simply arbitrary. We can chart a pattern of regular causality while leaving open the possibility that the creator of order can in principle vary it. This allows the complex structure of finite being as uncovered by science to be a sign of God's wisdom, without in any way seeing creation as a necessary outworking or development of divine being. Furthermore, the order of finite being, a theme very prominent in Islamic exegesis, is a sign not only of wisdom but also of providential care because the ordering of creation brings benefits to humanity. Creation is not simply a beautiful and harmonious structure; it is a structure focused upon the human, who has a unique position in creation as vicegerent of God and as the one who can articulate God's praise. Christianity, especially later Greek patristic thought as found in someone like Maximus the Confessor, likewise sees the human intelligence as what creation is working toward, and sees that intelligence itself as having a mediatorial function, a "priestly" role in bringing the meaning of creation to speech. Order, in other words, is not just something to be contemplated but is something that involves the human agent.

In this perspective, of course, knowledge has to be thought of in a many-layered fashion. Knowledge is certainly the awareness of the facts of a material environment, understood as fully as possible. This knowledge has elements of absolute clarity about it when mathematical reasoning is involved, but it is also corrigible: disagreement is unavoidable. But to know all this does not deliver what the believer considers the more significant kind of knowing, which is what arises (for the Christian) from sharing by grace in the act that sustains the finite world, or (for the Muslim) from recognizing in creation the presence of a causeless good will that demands obedient adoration (God has freely chosen these possibilities over those so that the world may be maximally adapted to human welfare). Revelation is not in any way a rival to reason on either scheme but the sheer making-known by God's free historical act in incarnation or scripture of his eternal good will, his choice to be known to (and in) what he has made.

This is relevant to one particular set of problems that has cropped up in the modern era for both faiths. If revelation is decisive and comprehensive, should not the media of revelation convey true propositions about the finite world? Or, in plain terms, should we not expect scripture to give us "scientific" information? And if so, is not the presence of such information in scripture long before any secular science confirmed it a clear proof of the divine origin of scripture? It is interesting to see that medieval Islamic scholars were already cautioning against this as an apologetic move—partly on the grounds that it was not the business of scripture to decide uncertain issues in the structure of finite being, and partly because of the implied confusion of different sorts of knowledge implied in the argument. The issue is still a current one, given the considerable amount of popular apologetic claiming Qur'ānic authority for various discoveries about the beginnings of the universe or the structure of material reality or human origins. It is paralleled by the Christian fundamentalist endeavor both to find biblical analogues to specific scientific doctrines and to demonstrate gaps in scientific evidence or reasoning that scriptural evidence can fill. Most mainstream thinkers in both traditions would be wary of this blurring of categories. The underlying question is, what does revelation "need" to provide us with? A revelation that included quasi-scientific information might well be thought a puzzling matter in that it gave knowledge that was in principle accessible by other means. One could appeal to the evidential force of information miraculously provided long before "natural" means could have attained to it, but the effect is actually, if paradoxically, to subordinate revelation to science, as if the evidences of revelation had to wait until science had confirmed them. The basic agreement in classical Islamic and Christian thought about the difference between levels or modes of knowing remains a surer guide.

Knowing is essentially an effective contact with truth. Truth is one, indeed, but that does not mean that it is known in one mode: the truth of a matter of contingent fact is established by various means, which we learn as we learn our languages; the truth of ethical principle may be as firmly established but the means by which we learn it are not the same as those for contingent facts;

the truth involved in understanding another person's temperament or qualities requires different methods again and different processes of learning. And this is perhaps the key point. "Scientific method" is thought of (not very accurately) as a coherent and accessible thing that can be learned by methods available to everyone. Other kinds of learning that take for granted a substantial passage of time and involvement with a community of other learners and teachers look less "open." The Enlightenment suspicion of authority that is not instantly open to inspection by universal criteria makes people unwilling to take seriously the more varied and humanly complex kinds of learning that operate outside what are thought to be straightforward scientific disciplines. Recent discussion of the supposed "science and religion debate" has certainly made it clear that a good many spokesmen for scientific method have fallen into the trap of supposing that even within the sciences there is one privileged set of methods, with the effect of reducing less "exact" disciplines to the terms of the more "exact" ones, so that a rather old-fashioned model of mechanistic physics is implicitly presented as the only truly robust scientific discourse. But once we recognize that scientific disciplines themselves work in diverse ways, we shall be less likely to import the mythology of a single kind of real or "hard" knowledge into other areas of human learning. If there is a debate between religion and science, it should certainly not be cast in these terms.

Is there in fact such a debate at all? Most of the contributors to this book would be very skeptical—and very critical—of both incautious scientists and ill-informed believers who have perpetuated the idea of some inherent collision. Not least, they are able to point to the undoubted influence in scientific development of precisely the metaphysic of consistent finite causality ardently promoted by Jews, Muslims, and Christians alike, and to the bare fact of the quality of scientific work done by religious believers of all traditions. But there is an issue here, not so much about science and faith as about a lazy secular culture that is in a large number of ways reducing what we understand as knowledge by quantifying and functionalizing it. And underlying this is the much more serious question of the construction of the "modern" self—preoccupied with autonomy, embarrassed about solidarities—the self that is increasingly being promoted in education, entertainment, and even secular law. The significance of this colloquium is in part that scholars from both religious traditions have identified together some of the reasons for thinking that the supposed debate between religion and science is a fiction and have also identified together some of the fundamental concerns in the contemporary world about knowing and learning. If it were not (because of unhelpful current usage) a misleading phrase, you could say that we share a humanist agenda—humanist in the old sense of a perspective informed by deep cultural resources that are themselves rooted in a conviction about the dignity and tragic possibilities of human persons in their standing before God. That kind of humanism is the opposite of secularism, which, in denying the religious perspective, denies at the same time the full dimensions of humanity. As Muslims and Christians have consistently taught and believed, the denial of God is ultimately what C. S. Lewis called "the abolition of man" as well.

None of this means any diminution of the achievements of experimental science—both in the great period of scientific flowering that medieval Islam and then later Renaissance Christendom witnessed, and in the last century or so. The idea that a refusal of the task of inquiry and adaptation is a sort of betrayal of faith is one that needs reaffirming. It is a betrayal of faith to the extent that it suggests that revealed religion has cause to be fearful of experimental discovery of the truth. We have made that mistake in the past often enough, but it is time to put it decisively behind us, as the address by Pope John Paul II in this volume eloquently argues. On the contrary, the scientific enterprise is now to be welcomed and recognized as a matter of celebration, as part of that sense of how the wisdom and providence of God may be touched or shared by us. And if we are indeed living in an era in which what I have called humanism is under threat in a global culture of market values and individual agendas, it is crucial that Islam and Christianity, and the other great religious traditions as well, reinforce in each other all that makes for effective resistance to a "scientism" and a functionalism that obscure human dignity. The Christian and Islamic approach to the rational and ordered cosmos is one in which both divine and human freedom have a crucial role, the latter generated by the former. That finite but authentic freedom, the freedom of persons in relation, is something we can and must celebrate and defend together—as we found ourselves doing, with much relish, in our days together in Istanbul.

Index

Arabic names beginning with the article "al-" or the article "el-" are found under the first significant element; thus, al-Ghazālī is alphabetized as G. Arabic names beginning with Ibn, such as Ibn Rushd, are alphabetized as I.